The Scarecrow Author Bibliographies

WILKIE COLLINS

An Annotated Bibliography,

1889-1976

by

KIRK H. BEETZ

The Scarecrow Author Bibliographies, No. 35

The Scarecrow Press, Inc.
Metuchen, N.J. & London
1978

My thanks to Elliot Gilbert, professor of English,
for his assistance and encouragement, and for providing me with the time I needed.

Library of Congress Cataloging in Publication Data

Beetz, Kirk H., 1952-
    Wilkie Collins : an annotated bibliography,
1889-1976.

    (The Scarecrow author bibliographies ; no. 35)
    Includes indexes.
    1. Collins, Wilkie, 1824-1889--Bibliography.
Z8184.6.B43 [PR4496]   016.823'8   77-26609
ISBN 0-8108-1103-0

I dedicate this book to Sue Munich, who, like the author, loves a well written story.

CONTENTS

INTRODUCTION

The contents of this bibliography are organized in such a manner that one can easily find works in either a general or a specific area. For example, if one seeks firsthand accounts of Collins, one would look in Part II (Criticism and Scholarship) of the bibliography proper, under BOOKS 1 and 2.a and PERIODICALS 1. If the categories into which this bibliography is divided do not meet one's desires, then one should consult the Subject Index. This index is conceived as purely supplemental to the established categories--William H. Marshall's Wilkie Collins, for instance, is a book which evaluates the whole of Collins's literary corpus; thus, it is not cited under "novels" in the index, since its status as a book devoted solely to Collins already establishes its content.

The annotations serve as guides to the contents of the works listed. They should not be viewed as definitive--instead, they are attempts to indicate the essence. Most of the evaluative comments in the annotations summarize the scholars' opinions of given works, although I do include educated opinions of my own.

Since Collins's career is still misunderstood by many scholars, a short bibliographical essay along historical lines is included in the present work. The essay is not intended to be definitive, but rather a quick reference source providing both student and scholar with the background behind the writing and publication of specific works by Collins, and behind his career in general. This essay, comprised of numbered paragraphs, is provided with its own index, which refers to these numbers.

Please note that each discrete edition of Collins's works is given its own separate numbered entry. Strictly reprints however are listed together under the edition being reprinted. Each of Collins's works is given as a separate heading under its most common published title, and its first publication date is cited. (Bibliographic details can be checked in the Bibliographic Essay, via its Index.) After that heading, the editions of the given work are listed chronologically, with changes in titles and subtitles noted.

Good critical editions of Collins's works are hard to come by. As a result, scholarly and critical references to Collins's works are chaotic. The Chatto and Windus collected works (entry 1) seems to be preferred for textual reliability, but is scarce and hard to obtain for use. The Harper and Brothers collected works (entry 31) is referred to most often, but is nowhere near complete. The Collier edition (entry 49) is the most readily available of the collected works, and thus is increasingly referred to. Unfortunately, none of these editions of Collins's works is complete--and none of the texts is of the level of reliability that scholars usually require.

Of Collins's major novels, only two have had much bibliographical attention: The Moonstone and The Woman in White. The best texts of these works seem to be--and these are my personal preferences--the Penguin Books edition of The Moonstone (entry 177) as edited by J. I. M. Stewart, and the Houghton Mifflin Company's Riverside edition (entry 251) of The Woman in White, the text of which was established by Anthea Trodd on what appears to be a sound critical basis. The Woman in White has had much scholarly attention of late, and the versions edited by Julian Symons (entry 253) and Harvey Peter Sucksmith (entry 254) may be of critical interest.

The basic biography is still Kenneth Robinson's Wilkie Collins: A Biography (entry 370). Although more biographical material has come to light since Robinson's book appeared, the amount has not been enough to diminish its usefulness. The only introductory critical work--fortunately, it is a good one--is William H. Marshall's Wilkie Collins (entry 368). Again, although the work of Peter Caracciolo (entry 567), U. C. Knoepflmacher (entry 448), and others has been opening up new critical horizons in the study of Collins, Marshall's book still covers the essentials of Collins's art, and remains a solid, well thought-out work.

Finally, one should note that this bibliography is selective in the sense that trivial references to Collins have been left out. The book reviews were chosen on the basis of their content about Collins. Many works were read which are not included in the listings. It is hoped, though, that everything of importance is included.

WILKIE COLLINS'S WORKS, 1843-1890:
A BIBLIOGRAPHIC ESSAY*

1. The earliest published work by Wilkie Collins traced with any certainty is "The Last Stage Coachman," which was published in August 1843 by the Illuminated Magazine, when Collins was nineteen years old. The next known work is Memoirs of the Life of William Collins, Esq., R. A. (London: Longman, Brown, Green, and Longmans), published in 1848. This biography of Wilkie's father offers hints of the diligence and imagery which marks Collins's mature work. Although the book is written in a workmanlike manner, Collins leaves out much of human interest. He instead writes lengthy descriptions of his father's paintings, and demonstrates a descriptive talent which is an asset in his future works, but makes the biography a slow, sometimes cumbersome, affair.

2. The sales of the book were in the hundreds, enough to give Collins a feeling of gratification--and relief. The book had been a duty, and even though Wilkie's affection for his stern father is revealed in the biography, it reads as if it were a duty.

3. The next significant publication for Wilkie Collins was the February 1850 production of Antonina: or, The Fall of Rome. This novel was Collins's first and last attempt to write historical fiction. The necessity of altering the historical facts of a morally decaying Rome in order to suit Victorian moral standards inhibited Collins, and went against his meticulous writing style. The conversations between characters, and the plotting are both representative of an imma-

---

*Works of primary importance in writing this essay were items (entries) 421, 424, 427, 490 and 591. The paragraphs in this essay are numbered and the special index immediately following refers to these numbers.

ture writer.   Perhaps of greatest significance is the influence
his circle of artist friends exerted on the book.   None other
than John Ruskin took an interest in the book, although it is
unclear whether Ruskin's influence ultimately played a part
in the book's publication (in three volumes by Richard Bentley, of London).   Ruskin to a small extent, and John Everett
Millais, E. M. Ward, and other future members of the Pre-
Raphaelite Brotherhood, as well as other artists, provided
much of the support for Wilkie's early work.   They presented
Collins's work in many important quarters.   Later in the
nineteenth century, Wilkie Collins, as the enormously popular writer of sensation fiction, returned the support with
unfailing generosity.

        4.   In January 1851, Richard Bentley published Col-
lins's Rambles Beyond Railways: or, Notes in Cornwall
Taken A-Foot, the single-volume account of an 1850 summer
holiday hike through Cornwall.   The sales of Rambles Beyond
Railways and of Antonina encouraged Wilkie.   Later in life,
he was bemused by the insistence of some critics that he was
a historical novelist, even though from 1851 onward his popularity rested on what Victorians called "sensation" fiction.

        5.   Augustus Egg, a painter, introduced Wilkie Col-
lins to Charles Dickens, who was already familiar with Collins's work, in March 1851.   This contact, in the form of
the procuring of a part for Collins in Dickens's production of
Bulwer-Lytton's comedy, Not So Bad as We Seem, developed
into an intimate friendship which lasted until Dickens's death
in 1870.   Whatever Dickens's influence on Collins's art, or
Collins's influence on Dickens's art--two heavily debated
topics--Dickens clearly had an affect on Collins.

        6.   Collins published a few stories in Bentley's Mis-
cellany in 1851 and 1852.   In early 1852, he tried to sell
"The Monkstons of Wincot Abbey" to Household Words, the
magazine edited by Dickens (Kenneth Robinson, on page 73
of Wilkie Collins--entry 370--dates this story as early 1853;
the dating used here is from R. V. Andrew's "A Wilkie Collins Check-List"--entry 518).   The story, also known as
"Mad Monkton," deals with hereditary insanity, a subject too
touchy for Dickens's magazine.   It was published in Fraser's
Magazine in late 1855, and was reprinted as "Brother Griffith's Story of Mad Monkton" in The Queen of Hearts, 1859.

        7.   On April 24, 1852, Collins sold his first story,
"A Terribly Strange Bed," to Household Words (the story

later appeared in After Dark, 1856).   The story has enjoyed
a lasting popularity, and still appears in short story anthologies.

    8.   The publication of Basil: A Story of Modern Life
in three volumes by Richard Bentley in November of 1852
marks a considerable advancement in the novel-craft of Collins.   He creates characters which can interest readers, and
successfully establishes atmospheres which play upon a reader's emotions.   Intimations of the social reform themes
which mark his last novels can be found in Basil.

    9.   Wilkie Collins was plagued from Basil onward by
piracy in the United States.   Eventually, he arranged with
Harper and Brothers to forward to them advance proofs of
novels serialized in Dickens's Household Words and All the
Year Round, so that Harper's Weekly or Harper's Monthly
could publish the novels in America simultaneously with
British publication.   Harper and Brothers would beat the
pirates to book publication by weeks, and thus garner the
initial sales of Collins's works.   In exchange for the early
proofs, Harper and Brothers paid Collins for each novel.   In
spite of the big advantage Harper and Brothers had, pirates
--publishing in a nation with lax copyright laws--sold untold
quantities of Collins's books, sometimes numbering in the
hundreds of thousands.

    10.   After the publication of Basil, Wilkie Collins's
production slowed.   In the early spring of 1853 he wrote
"Gabriel's Marriage," a short story published in two April
issues of Household Words.   Collins, Charles Dickens, and
Augustus Egg spent the summer anticipating a journey through
Italy.   Collins also wrote most of a new novel.   The men
spent the better part of October and well into December in
travel, and both Collins and Egg spent more money than they
could afford.

    11.   Collins began 1854 by completing the novel he
started in 1853.   Entitled Hide and Seek, it was published in
three volumes by Richard Bentley, and was a marked con-
trast to Basil.   Where the latter novel was somber, humor-
less, and an unrelenting tragedy, the former (in later editions entitled, Hide and Seek: or, The Mystery of Mary
Grice) was tender and contained some of Collins's most successful early attempts at humor.

    12.   Hide and Seek represents a step toward a more

detached view of the events he rendered in fiction. Basil is
viewed in many critical discussions as an autobiographical
work.   How much of it represents Wilkie Collins himself is
still unclear.   Hide and Seek is less of an interior work, and
has a broader view of the world.   The traits of Collins's mature work become more clear.   Mental and emotional disease
and injury are paralleled by physical deformities--and often
the physically deformed seem more whole than their society
and the handsome people around them.   Heroes and heroines
must defy society--which becomes increasingly oppressive in
Collins's works--in order to achieve their goals and find any
degree of happiness.

13.   Also, Collins's war with the general world of
critics begins in earnest with Hide and Seek.   In Basil he included a preface which addressed the reader in a friendly
fashion.   Against almost all advice, including that of Dickens,
Collins persisted in including prefaces addressing the readers
in his novels.   These prefaces grew more hostile toward critics with each succeeding novel.   Basil had been assaulted by
the more prurient critics as immoral.   Collins showed signs
of being offended by the criticism of this remarkably frank
portrayal of adultery and his discussions of sexual relationships.   His clearly antisocial viewpoint in Basil antagonized
many.   In Hide and Seek, however, he showed he had learned
to coat his antisocial views with a gloss of good humor and
interesting language.   In spite of his growing reputation, however, and of his increasing notoriety, Hide and Seek did not
sell well, although the publisher did barely sell the first
printing.

14.   The study of the bibliography of Collins becomes
more complex after Hide and Seek; he begins collaborating
with Dickens.   Late in his life Wilkie would comment with
amusement on those critics who persisted in claiming for
Dickens a story or paragraph by Collins, and claiming for
Collins work written by Dickens.   Even three-quarters of the
way into the twentieth century, the questions of authorship sur-
rounding their joint ventures have not all been satisfactorily
answered.   Add to this the tendency of pirate publishers and
ill-informed scholars to assign works not written by either to
each of the two men, and to publish works by one under the
other's name, and the confusion can be great.

15.   The Seven Poor Travellers was one such collaboration between the two men.   Each year Dickens would produce
an extra Christmas number of his magazine.   In 1854 he asked

Collins, now a close friend, to help him with the special
December issue.   Clearly, Collins did contribute a portion
of the special issue.   According to M. L. Parrish (page 24
of Wilkie Collins and Charles Reade, entry 430) six of the
issue's eight parts are by Collins.   R. V. Andrew (page 79
of "A Wilkie Collins Check-List," entry 518) credits five
chapters of Collins, and possibly one other, including Chapter
IV, "A Stolen Letter."   This story was reprinted in After
Dark (1856), and even though it bears a resemblance to Edgar
Allan Poe's "The Purloined Letter," has had an enduring
popularity.

16.   The year 1855 represents the beginning of Collins's
full-time devotion to writing.   Although he was always a devoted worker, writing began to be an obsession.   He wrote
"Sister Rose," The Lighthouse, "The Yellow Mask," and "The
Cruise of the Tom-Tit," and contributed to the special Christmas number of Household Words.

17.   "Sister Rose" was reprinted in a single volume
in the United States, in 1855, and was attributed to Charles
Dickens.   It appears in Collins's After Dark (1856) and is
certainly Collins's work.   The Lighthouse was written for
one of Dickens's amateur stage productions, was well-re-
ceived and was professionally produced in 1857 at the Olympic Theatre.   The two-act drama was not published.   "The
Yellow Mask" appeared in the July issues of Household Words,
and had a large following of readers well into the twentieth
century.   It was reprinted in After Dark (1856) under the title,
"The Professor's Story of the Yellow Mask."   The special
Christmas number of Dickens's magazine was entitled The
Holly Tree Inn, and included Collins's story, "The Ostler."
The story later appeared as "Brother Morgan's Story of the
Dream-Woman" in The Queen of Hearts (1859), and was expanded for Collins's tour of the United States.   The story
was the principal part of his program for public readings in
the United States, and brought forth outraged critical articles
in American newspapers, in which he was accused of nega-
tively affecting the "purity" of American women.   His un-
apologetic portraits of fallen women--that is, prostitutes,
adulteresses, and thieves--offended the critics during the
1873 trip.

18.   The publication of After Dark, a collection of
Wilkie Collins's short stories, in February began a momen-
tous year in Collins's publishing career.   The two-volume
collection included one new story, "The Lady of Glenwith

Grange, " and reprints of stories which first appeared in
periodicals, and was published by Smith, Elder, and Company
of London, who apparently had approached Collins sometime
earlier about the possibility.   The book received mixed reviews.

19.   Collins sold three more pieces of fiction, so far
as is currently known, in 1856--all to Household Words. Collins was a very determined business man, and he was well
aware of the need to keep his name before the public; hence
he insisted that his name appear with his work.   Therefore,
these stories probably are the extent of his new published
fiction in 1856, in addition to "The Lady of Glenwith Grange. "
This last story, along with "A Rogue's Life" (reprinted in one
volume in 1879 by Richard Bentley and Son, of London, as
A Rogue's Life: From His Birth to His Marriage) and The
Wreck of the Golden Mary, another special Christmas number
collaboration with Dickens, have each elicited a small amount
of critical and scholarly comment.   The other story, "Diary
of Anne Rodway, " was reprinted in The Queen of Hearts (1859)
under the title of "Brother Owen's Story of Anne Rodway. "
The bulk of Collins's publications for the year were journal-
istic articles for Household Words.

20.   The Wreck of the Golden Mary presents several
problems.   Bibliographers and scholars have had a tendency
to credit only Charles Dickens with authorship of this issue
of Household Words.   Reprints of The Wreck of the Golden
Mary are nearly always listed in the major reference works
only under Dickens's name, with no mention of Collins.   This
confusion of authorship is part of the bibliographic manifesta-
tion of the bitterly negative aspect of Collins's close social
and working relationship with Dickens.   Without doubt, Charles
Dickens was the greater genius, a great literary force of the
nineteenth century.   Consequently, Collins has been often
buried under the tremendous scholarly interest in Dickens.
Collins did not improve his place in history by spurning critics and scholars, and asserting that the sales of his books
were evaluation enough for him.   In the case of The Wreck
of the Golden Mary, Collins wrote two of the three chapters,
"The Beguilement in the Boats" and "The Deliverance, " and
part of the first chapter, "The Wreck. "   The inspiration may
have been Dickens's, but most of the words are Collins's.

21.   Toward the end of the summer of 1856, Dickens
apparently recognized that Household Words was investing a
great deal of money in Collins's work.   He suggested to W. H.

Wills, his sub-editor (assistant editor in modern parlance)
that Wilkie be added to the magazine's staff. He saw in Wilkie a colleague receptive to suggestions and a reliable writer.
However, Wilkie, ever a hard bargainer, balked at the suggestion that he follow custom as a salaried staff member and
allow his articles to be published unsigned. He wanted his
name to be attached to all his articles and to be allowed to
serialize a full-length novel in the magazine. Dickens refused
to alter the custom of leaving staff contributions unsigned, but
did concede to Collins's desire to publish a serialized novel,
and agreed to advertise Collins's name before the start of
any "long story" by Collins. So far as is known, Collins accepted the compromise proposal.

22. In January 1857, The Dead Secret began its serialization in Household Words, and concluded in the middle of
June, six months later. It was written week by week, and
followed much the same pattern as Hide and Seek. Immediately upon completion, the novel was published in two volumes
by Bradbury and Evans of London. While writing this novel
from week to week, a very difficult task, Collins found time
to write a pair of short stories, one published in Harper's
Weekly, and the other in The National Magazine.

23. Also in January of 1857, Collins's play, The
Frozen Deep, was produced as one of Dickens's amateur productions. The play was later revised and printed in 1866
and produced by the Olympic Theatre. Even though the play
did well in 1857, its professional run in 1866 was unsuccessful. The play is of scholarly interest because it inspired the
idea for Dickens's A Tale of Two Cities. R. L. Brannan has
also used the 1857 version of the play as an example of
Dickens's approaches to drama in Under the Management of
Charles Dickens (entry 261).

24. Collins later adapted the play to narrative form,
and published it in Temple Bar, in 1874. He wrote the narrative form during his tour of the United States, and read it
publicly in February 1874, and was well received. It was
reprinted in The Frozen Deep and Other Stories, in two volumes, by Richard Bentley and Son. It also appeared under
the title of Readings in America (Hunter, Rose and Company,
1874).

25. Once he finished The Dead Secret, Collins em-
barked on other assignments for Household Words. He wrote
several articles and stories, including "The Lazy Tour of

Two Idle Apprentices" and the special Christmas issue, The
Perils of Certain English Prisoners--both in collaboration with
Dickens.   The former article stemmed from Dickens's desire
to get away from home for awhile.   He asked Collins for some
ideas for combining work with escape, and Collins came up
with a walking tour of Cumberland.   "The Lazy Tour" was
just that, and the account of their uneventful trip is padded
with reflections and a pair of short excursions into the macabre by Collins and Dickens.   Collins's macabre "The Double-
Bedded Room" reappears in The Queen of Hearts (1859) as
"Brother Morgan's Story of the Dead Hand. "

        26.   The Perils of Certain English Prisoners is a
more successful collaboration.   Again, the idea was Wilkie's,
and it is a melodrama of adventure in Central America.   Even
though the correspondence of Dickens and Collins in later
years indicates their belief that each could match the other's
style so as to be indistinguishable, one from the other, Collins's chapter, "The Prison in the Woods, " differs stylistically
from Dickens's two chapters.   Both "The Lazy Tour" and
Perils of Certain English Prisoners suffer, to a lesser extent,
from the same problems which plague the bibliographic study
of The Wreck of the Golden Mary.

        27.   By 1857, Collins had gained a surprising amount
of prestige.   With only his immature work behind him, Collins was nonetheless ranked by Edmund Yates in the second
number of The Train, as the fourth best living novelist in
England, behind only Charles Dickens, William Makepeace
Thackeray, and Charlotte Brontë.

        28.   In 1858, Collins increased his production of arti-
cles, writing at least seventeen.   The articles are interesting
primarily for their bold tone; Collins rails against social in-
justice, and shows the same sympathy for those given short
shrift in Victorian society and much of Victorian literature
that he shows in his fiction.   His outrage is sometimes vitu-
perative.   The background for his late work--usually viewed
as his inferior work--becomes more evident.   He is unquestionably disturbed by social injustices.   In his best work, his
concern manifests itself in strong female characters, often
homely and sometimes lower class--both are characteristics
that defy novel convention of the mid-Victorian era--and in
subtle conflicts between social outcasts and society.

        29.   Only four works of fiction by Collins are known
to have been published in 1858.   Chief among these are "Who

Is the Thief?" in the April issue of The Atlantic Monthly,
and A House to Let, the last special Christmas number of
Household Words on which Collins and Dickens collaborated.
Of greater interest is "Who Is the Thief?" which was included
in The Queen of Hearts (1859) under the title "Brother Griffith's Story of the Biter Bit," and is frequently referred to
as "The Biter Bit." The Story was extremely popular, and
appears in anthologies to this day. It has been praised for
its plot, its atmosphere, and its characterizations, and is
often ranked as one of Collins's best.

30.   Collins was occupied primarily by his journalis-
tic chores in 1859.   Except for one insignificant short story
published in January, his fiction ventures came in the last
months of the year.   The Queen of Hearts, which features
stories from Collins's periodical publications, was published
in three volumes by Hurst and Blackett of London in October,
and in one volume by Harper and Brothers of New York, also
in October.   In December, Collins contributed a story, "The
Ghost in the Cupboard Room" (reprinted as "'Blow Up with
the Brig!'" in Miss or Mrs. ?, 1873, and as "'Blow Up with
the Brig!': A Sailor's Story" in After Dark: And Other
Stories, 1875), to the special Christmas issue of Dickens's
new magazine, All the Year Round.

31.   Charles Dickens had a dispute with the publishers
of Household Words, Bradbury and Evans, in early 1959.   He
left the editorship of the magazine and founded All the Year
Round.   Bradbury and Evans launched a new magazine, Once
a Week, and a subscription war followed, as the two magazines battled for the readers of the defunct Household Words.
Dickens launched his new magazine with A Tale of Two Cities,
and he wanted a strong serialized novel to follow it.   He
asked his close friend, Wilkie Collins, to supply the needed
novel, in the hope that Collins's reliable prose would hold
the readers gained by A Tale of Two Cities.

32.   Wilkie Collins provided The Woman in White.
The novel began in the November issue of All the Year Round
and ended in August of 1860.   The serial was enormously
popular.   Crowds mobbed the offices of the magazine, eagerly
snatching up each new issue.   Parlor games quickly developed,
in which the object was to guess the content of the next section of The Woman in White.

33.   In the United States, Harper and Brothers ran
the novel in Harper's Weekly.   Early proofs of the novel were

sent by steamer across the Atlantic Ocean, and each installment was published simultaneously with the installment in
All the Year Round. The pirate publishers in the United
States eagerly prepared editions of the novel under their own
imprints. Harper and Brothers captured the early sales by
publishing a one-volume version of the novel before the month
of August was finished. Even so, the pirates were quickly
out with their own versions. In England, Sampson Low, Son,
and Company, of London, outbid their rivals for the right to
publish the book, and produced a three-volume version in August.

     34.   The proliferation of the novel was immense.
Throughout the rest of his life, Collins would periodically
receive notice of a new translation of the book into a non-
English language. As it was, The Woman in White quickly
appeared in German, French, Italian, Russian, and other
languages. Like other Victorian writers, Collins gained a
wide following in Russia. Unlike others, his books were sub-
sequently published in Asian languages and circulated in nearly
every literate nation of the world. Even late in the twentieth
century new versions of his books appeared in an Arabic dia-
lect. With the publication of The Woman in White, demand
for his previous books rose. Pirates scrambled to put out
their versions of Collins's works--some were odd slappings
together of stories and articles--and some books never written by Collins appeared with his name on them. In Leipzig,
Germany, Baron Bernhard Tauchnitz, who had quietly arranged
for the rights to all Continental European English language
publications of Collins's work years before, found his long
friendship with the novelist paying off. After The Woman in
White his investment in Collins's work was repaid many times
over.

     35.   The novel went through several editions in the
first few weeks after it was published. Authorized publishers
and pirates alike earned huge profits. In the United States
the pirates--whose records are not clear--evidently sold hundreds of thousands of cheap volumes. After The Woman in
White, Collins would point to his sales and ask whether the
critics or his huge public judged his work correctly. When
an antagonistic critic would point out that his works attracted
an audience of uneducated people (including illiterates who
pooled their spare moneys to pay someone to read Collins's
novels to their gatherings), he remained unruffled. He took
pleasure in appealing to both illiterates and the educated elite.
Gladstone, Thackeray, and others reported being unable to
put down The Woman in White.

36. Collins added a further complication for his bibliographers by tinkering with The Woman in White after it
was published in volume form. He was deeply concerned with
the precision of his plots, so he refined and corrected the
novel even after it had gone through more than one edition.
Unfortunately, his letters to Dickens, with whom he discussed
the novel's content, were destroyed by Dickens along with all
of the correspondence Dickens had collected. In a large bon-
fire Dickens burnt uncounted letters, not only from Collins,
but from many other writers.

37. Since he need never worry about earning a living
again--for publishers would pay what he demanded for the
rest of his life--and he disliked journalism, Collins left Dickens's staff. Illness created severe problems for him, so
Collins contributed only to the Christmas number of All the
Year Round, another collaboration with Dickens in 1860.

38. In 1861, Collins only published a couple of articles and contributed to the Christmas number of All the
Year Round. However, he began No Name that year, and it
began its serialization in a March issue of All the Year Round.
Collins was determined not to fall on his face after the enormous success of The Woman in White. He produced a strikingly different work. No Name is a didactic work, critical
of the inheritance laws of the United Kingdom; and it is the
most successful of his overtly didactic works. His public
bought up the issues of All the Year Round in which it appeared. Sampson Low, Son, and Company met the highest
bid for the novel, and secured the right to publish the book.
They produced a three-volume version in December 1862.
In spite of its arrangement with Collins, Harper and Brothers
was not able to beat its competitors to publication, but did
produce a one-volume version of No Name in 1863. No Name
went through several editions. Collins quickly wrote a dramatic version of No Name in five acts, which was not staged.
He himself published it as a four-act drama in 1870.

39. Publishers were eager to cash in on Collins's
popularity. Unauthorized dramatic versions of his novels
appeared on stage in both the United States and Britain--
these unauthorized dramas irritated Collins for the rest of
his life. Most of his short stories were reprinted in book
form by 1863. However, Collins's nonfiction articles had not
been reprinted. Thus, in the autumn of 1863, Sampson Low,
Son, and Company published My Miscellanies in two volumes.
The book was a collection of articles originally written for
Household Words and All the Year Round.

40.   Wilkie Collins did not apply himself to writing
again until 1864.   He began a novel, Armadale, in the spring,
and had a substantial portion of it completed by the time it
began its run in the November issue of The Cornhill Magazine.
In the United States, the novel was serialized in Harper's
Monthly.   The Civil War had brought about a severe drop in
the magazine's circulation.   Armadale helped increase the
magazine's circulation substantially.   When the very long
novel was published in volume form in 1866, it sold very
well.   Smith, Elder and Company of London brought out a
two-volume version in Britain, and Harper and Brothers
brought out a single-volume version in the United States.

41.   Collins found and held a large audience for his
works with the elements of sensation and an engaging prose
style.   In the space of seven years he wrote three novels,
each of which is strikingly dissimilar to the others.   Each
novel increased the circulation of the magazine which serialized it, and, in spite of Collins's demands for substantial
payments, the book editions made profits for their publishers.

42.   Collins wrote a dramatic version of Armadale in
1866.   This version was not produced or printed.   Collins
later rewrote the drama, and it was produced at the Globe
Theatre in 1876, under the title of Miss Gwilt.   Also in 1866,
The Frozen Deep (1857) was revised and produced at the
Olympic Theatre.

43.   In 1867, Collins collaborated with Charles Dickens on the Christmas number of All the Year Round.   They
wrote a story of adventure in the Alps, No Thoroughfare.
The magazine version is in "Acts" instead of chapters.   Parts
of Acts I and IV, and all of Act II, are by Collins.   The
dramatic version of the story appeared at the Adelphi Theatre
in December 1867, coinciding with the magazine publication.
Since Dickens was in the United States in late 1867, Collins
handled the necessary revisions of the stage script.   The
play ran for nearly seven months.   The great success of
this drama may well have encouraged Collins to adapt other
of his fiction to dramatic form.

44.   During 1867 Collins began work on The Moonstone.
This novel, along with The Woman in White, became, by the
turn of the century, the novel regarded as most representative
of Wilkie Collins at his best.   It is a remarkably well-knit
story, and its plot and inventions, like those of The Woman
in White, have been imitated ad infinitum.   What were new

themes and motifs in The Moonstone are now the commonplace
of the detective novel.   Yet this remarkable original, complex, and tightly written novel was, for the most part, written while Collins was in terrible pain and deeply under the
influence of laudanum--a tincture of opium.

45.   When The Moonstone began its run in January
1868 in All the Year Round--boosting the magazine's sagging
circulation--Collins was struck by a terrible attack of a disease called "rheumatic gout. "   His eyes swelled with blood,
and his joints became nearly immobile.   Since his novel had
begun its run, Collins refused to take any time off from writing.   He was a meticulous worker, who took pride in the constant praise of his American, German (Tauchnitz), and
British publishers, all of whom appreciated his diligence and
the punctual manuscripts.   Thus, he hired secretaries to take
the dictation of his novel.   His groans and cries were so un-
nerving that several male secretaries were unable to stay
with him.   Eventually a woman took up the pen for Collins and was able to ignore his suffering.   The laudanum
took its toll.   Upon reading the conclusion of The Moonstone, after he was recovering, Collins was delighted with
the writing, but did not recognize the work as his own.   The
disease had interfered with his work in the past, and would
in the future--sometimes forcing him to delay completion of
work past publishing deadlines.   To his credit, the delays
were surprisingly rare.

46.   Just as had happened with The Woman in White,
each installment of The Moonstone was eagerly anticipated.
The novel did better than Dickens's serialized work while
running in All the Year Round, and when published in volume
form, outsold Dickens's work.   The Moonstone's success
seems to have strained the relationship between Dickens and
Collins.   Dickens's The Mystery of Edwin Drood (1870), may
well have been an attempt to outdo Collins at Collins's own
game.

47.   The Tinsley Brothers, a small London publishing
house, published the British version of The Moonstone in
three volumes in 1868.   William Tinsley, the publisher, and
Collins disputed over both payment and the conditions under
which second and subsequent imprints would be issued.   Tinsley lost Collins's future business.   In the United States, the
pirates brought out their unauthorized editions simultaneously
with the Harper and Brothers edition.   The pirates had the
advantage of lower prices, but Harper and Brothers had the

best text.   Even though the pirates apparently captured a
huge share of the market, Harper and Brothers did well by
the novel, which they published in one volume.

48.   In 1869, Collins collaborated with his friend,
Charles Fechter, the actor, on a play, Black and White.   The
play was printed by C. Whiting of London, in one volume.
It was produced at the Adelphi Theatre in March of 1869, and
ran there for nearly six weeks before it toured outside of
London.   Also in 1869, Collins's novel Man and Wife began
its serialization in the December 11 issue of Harper's Weekly.
The Novel began its British serialization in January of 1870,
in Cassell's Magazine.

49.   Man and Wife is sometimes marked as the start-
ing point of the decline in the quality of Wilkie Collins's fiction.   His popularity--contrary to an early twentieth-century
myth--never waned, but his work became increasingly concerned with social reform and his plots, while still good,
never equalled the plots of the four novels written from 1859
to 1868.   Some critics see a cause and effect relationship
between the didactic content of Collins's work and the decline
in the artistic merit of that work.   However, Collins's best
work includes social comment and satire; and his steady decline in health, his dependence on huge daily doses of laudanum, the loss of the companionship of many of his friends
through estrangement or death or geographical separation, the
loss of the inspiration and aid of Charles Dickens--who died
in 1870--the influence of Charles Reade, and Collins's hor-
rible drug-induced hallucinations, all may have contributed to
his artistic decline.   Certainly Man and Wife is inferior to
The Moonstone.   The novel, which attacks Britain's obsession
with athleticism, and attacks Scottish marriage laws, was
usually not reviewed on its artistic merit, however.   It was
attacked, just as were many of Collins's works, as immoral.
To Collins's credit, he still wrote works ahead of their time.
Public opinion, years later, came to his way of thinking.

50.   F. S. Ellis of London, a publisher probably
brought into contact with Collins through his acquaintances in
the Pre-Raphaelite Brotherhood, brought out a three-volume
edition of Man and Wife in 1870.   Harper and Brothers brought
out a single-volume edition of it in 1870.   The first of Collins's outright propaganda novels, Man and Wife sold well, although his publishers complained that his expletives, such as
"damn, " might offend the public.   He allowed rare changes,
but usually refused to alter his expletives, arguing that in
order to be believable, characters must speak realistically.

51.   Collins wrote a four-act dramatic version of Man
and Wife.   It was published as Man and Wife: A Dramatic
Story in one volume by Collins, himself, in 1870.   It was
not until 1873 that the play was produced.   It ran for nearly
five months at the Prince of Wales Theatre.   In the United
States, Augustin Daly, among others, produced an unauthorized
dramatic version of the novel in 1871.

52.   The year of 1870 was an active one for Collins's
dramas.   In addition to writing Man and Wife, Collins published a four-act version of No Name.   Unhappy with this
version, he let Wybert Reeve (see entry 573) tinker with the
play.   Reeve seems to have performed the play in Australia.
R. V. Andrew (page 91 of "A Wilkie Collins Check-List,"
entry 518) records a production of the play at the Fifth
Avenue Theatre in New York in 1871.

53.   Collins also published a dramatic version of The
Woman in White in 1871, in one volume.   The play had been
tried out in the summer of 1870, but Collins found the drama
unsatisfactory.   Not until October of 1871 was the play produced.   It ran at the Olympic Theatre, where Collins met
Wybert Reeve, mentioned above.   The play ran for about five
months, then went on a tour of Britain which lasted a number
of years.

54.   The novel Poor Miss Finch was serialized in
Cassell's Magazine in 1871.   It was published by Richard
Bentley and Son of London in three volumes in 1872.   Harper
and Brothers published a one-volume version the same year.
The book is a bizarre story of a blind woman who falls in
love with one of twin brothers.   The other brother develops
an affection for her.   The brother she loves is an epileptic
who is treated with silver nitrate, and who, as a consequence,
turns blue.   The woman miraculously gains sight through a
wonderful medical operation by a German physician, and then
goes through much trauma in her love life.   Somehow, Collins contrives to make things seem to end well by having the
woman go blind again.

55.   Sometime in 1870 or 1871, Collins begins to
weary of his constant battles with pirates of his works in
foreign countries.   Tauchnitz in Germany seemed to over-
come the competition for English versions of Collins's work
in Continental Europe easily, but the authorized publishers
of translations of Collins's works were sometimes hard
pressed.   He managed--urgently--to persuade pirates in

Holland to pay him small gratuities for his work. Yet, the proliferation of his works continued and keeping up with his authorial rights was a strain on the now very ill Collins.

56. A long short story, "Miss or Mrs. ?," was published in The London Graphic Illustrated Newspaper in December of 1871. In 1873, the story formed the bulk of a book entitled Miss or Mrs. ?: And Other Stories in Outline in one volume by Richard Bentley and Son. Other stories in the book are "'Blow Up with the Brig!'" (originally "The Ghost in the Cupboard Room" in the Christmas number of All the Year Round, 1859) and "The Fatal Cradle" (originally "Picking Up Waifs at Sea" in the Christmas number of All the Year Round, 1861). From 1875 onward, "A Mad Marriage" (originally "A Fatal Fortune" in All the Year Round in October of 1874) was included in the book.

57. The New Magdalen, a novel, occupied Collins's attention through most of 1872. It ran from January through December in the magazine Temple Bar. In early 1873 the novel appeared in book form, published by Richard Bentley and Son in two volumes. In Toronto, Canada, the firm of Hunter, Rose and Company published a one-volume edition of the novel.

58. The book argues for a charitable view of human frailty. The central character is a reformed prostitute who undergoes various mistreatments at the hands of supposedly upright Christians. Seldom is Collins's dislike of social hypocrites so heavy-handedly expressed as it is in The New Magdalen. Collins was publicly assailed for his immorality--a prostitute, reformed or not, was not supposed to be a sympathetic character. Nonetheless, the novel was a popular success.

59. When the dramatic version of The New Magdalen opened at the Olympic Theatre, the audience received it enthusiastically. Wilkie was called onto the stage to take bows between acts. The play was quickly translated into Italian, French, Russian, German, and Dutch. It was a big success. The British version of the play was published in one volume by Collins in 1873.

60. Also in the early 1870's, Harper and Brothers began its attempt to publish an "Illustrated Library Edition" series of Collins's works. The texts in the series are of haphazard quality, but they form a collection some scholars still use as basic reference texts.

61.   In addition to the publications Miss or Mrs. ?
and The New Magdalen, "John Jago's Ghost" began publication
in December of 1873 in The Home Journal of London.   In the
United States, the story appeared under the title "The Dead
Alive" from December 1873 into January of 1874 in The New
York Fireside Companion.   It was reprinted as "John Jago's
Ghost" in The Frozen Deep and Other Stories, a two-volume
book published in 1874 by Richard Bentley and Son.

62.   During the autumn and winter of 1873, Collins
toured the United States, giving frequent readings.   He revised and expanded "The Dream Woman" (1855) for the public
readings.   The audience reception was good, but, as mentioned earlier, critics were very concerned about the story's
effect on the purity of American women.   While on the tour,
Collins adapted The Frozen Deep to narrative form, and
eventually read it in New York.   He and it were very well
received.   Temple Bar ran the narrative "The Frozen Deep"
in the late summer and autumn of 1874.   Both new versions
of "The Dream Woman" and "The Frozen Deep" were published by Hunter, Rose and Company in one volume, in 1874,
entitled Readings in America.   In addition to all this activity,
Collins found time to write a story, "A Fatal Fortune. "

63.   The year 1875 marks an important change in the
manner of publication of Collins's books.   Wilkie Collins had
long suffered from piracy, and had long taken pride in the
fact that people at all levels of social station enjoyed his
books.   He conceived the idea that cheap legitimate editions
of his works would sell every bit as well as the pirated edi-
tions--and, because of his popularity, would easily recoup
the money the publisher of such cheap editions would have to
pay him.   Thus, good reliable versions of his work might be
made available to the reader whose funds were small.   Apparently his regular publishers disliked the idea.

64.   Andrew Chatto, on the other hand, of the young
publishing firm of Chatto and Windus, of London, liked the
idea.   In 1875, the copyrights to Collins's works were trans-
ferred to Chatto and Windus, and the firm became his main
publisher.   Collins was right, and Chatto and Windus's "cheap
editions" sold well.

65.   The Law and the Lady ran in The London Graphic
in the spring of 1875, then quickly appeared in a three-volume Chatto and Windus edition.   Harper and Brothers, un-
convinced that they could outsell the pirates, produced its

usual one-volume version. In 1875, Collins also sold one
short story and wrote Miss Gwilt, a dramatic version of
Armadale (1864-1866). The play was produced in the spring
of 1876 at the Globe Theatre. It was controversial and did
well, although not as well as Collins's previous plays.

66.   The Two Destinies was published in Temple Bar
in 1876. It appeared in book form the same year: two volumes by Chatto and Windus, and one volume by Harper and
Brothers. Although Collins remained popular, this novel and
The Law and the Lady show a clear decline in his powers.
Even his carefully constructed prose, which once was engag-
ingly spontaneous, seems stiff in these novels. The year
1876 is otherwise marked only by the publication of a short
story.

67.   Collins wrote three short stories in 1877, chief
among which was "My Lady's Money. " It was published in
The London Illustrated News in late 1877. Bernhard Tauchnitz
combined it with another of the stories ("Mr. Percy and the
Prophet" in All the Year Round, July 1877) in a one-volume
book, entitled, appropriately enough, My Lady's Money and
Percy and the Prophet, in 1877. For once, Tauchnitz was
the first to publish one of Collins's works in book form. Harper and Brothers did not come out with its My Lady's Money:
An Episode in the Life of a Young Girl until 1878.

68.   The Moonstone was condensed into a four-act
drama and was produced at the Olympic Theatre in September 1877. That year is marked by Collins's increasingly
close friendship with Charles Reade and the increasing sever-
ity of his illness. Biographers and acquaintances alike have
marveled at his being able to write at all.

69.   In 1878, Collins wrote a pair of short stories,
and a novel, The Haunted Hotel. The novel appeared in The
Belgravia Magazine, then appeared in one-volume editions by
Rose-Belford Publishing Company of Toronto, and by Chatto
and Windus. The novel shows some of Collins's earlier artistic ability. It is a ghost story which transcends the conventions of the genre. Swinburne disliked it ("Wilkie Collins, "
1889, entry 546), but T. S. Eliot praised it ("Wilkie Collins
and Dickens, " 1927, entry 541). The novel was popular, and
was superior to Collins's recent work.

70.   Collins began a propaganda novel even before
The Haunted Hotel finished its serialization. The Fallen

Leaves--First Series ran in The World from 1878 into 1879,
and in The Canadian Monthly from 1879 into 1880.   Chatto
and Windus brought out a three-volume edition of the novel
in 1879.   The novel deals with a reformed prostitute and a
socialist.   The story seems designed to antagonize the critics.
The book did not sell badly--but it sold far below Collins's
usual standards.   Hence, a promised Second Series was not
written.

71.   The year 1879 saw the publication in book form
of A Rogue's Life (1856) by Richard Bentley and Son.   Collins adapted his play, The Red Vial (1858), into a novel
which ran in syndicated papers (R. V. Andrew's "A Wilkie
Collins Check-List," page 88, entry 518) and was published
in three volumes in 1880 by Chatto and Windus, under the
title Jezebel's Daughter.

72.   In late 1880, the novel The Black Robe began its
run in The Canadian Monthly.   Soon after it finished its serialization in the summer of 1881, Chatto and Windus published
a three-volume edition.   The novel's main character is a
Roman Catholic priest who plots to take over a valuable estate.
The book was very well received--even in predominantly Roman
Catholic countries, apparently--and was thought to be the best
of Collins's recent work.

73.   Collins wrote three stories and an article during
1881.   The big event of the year was his hiring of A. P.
Watt, a literary agent, to place his next book with a publisher.   After a time, Collins and Watt became friends.
Watt became Collins's permanent literary agent.

74.   From late summer 1882 until the summer of
1883, one of Collins's most controversial novels made its
serial run in The Belgravia Magazine.   The novel, Heart and
Science, was published in three volumes by Chatto and Windus
in 1883.   In it, Collins indulges his interest in science and
at the same time propagandizes against vivisection.   The book
elicited comment about its merit for years after Collins's
death.   Otherwise, 1882 is marked by a short story and a
chapter, "Recollections of Charles Fechter," contributed to
Charles Albert Fechter by Kate Field, and published by Osgood of Boston in the same year.

75.   In mid-1883, Collins's play Rank and Riches was
produced at the Adelphi Theatre.   Later in the year he had
a story published.   The play was a disaster.   Everyone

concerned had expected it to be a big success, so its failure
was all the more crushing than it might have been.   The
audience expressed its discontent loudly.   The opening scene
was laughed at, and the play was never given an opportunity
to develop.   The leading lady was laughed at until she cried.
The leading man, G. W. Anson, was so angered that he
berated the audience for its bad behavior.   The regular play-
goers in the audience never forgave him, and Anson was
eventually forced to leave England for Australia, because his
performances were so often interrupted.   The disaster essentially ended Collins's career as a playwright.   Interestingly,
Kenneth Robinson (page 306 of Wilkie Collins: A Biography,
entry 427) records that Rank and Riches did well in the United
States.

76.   One or two early scholars speculated that in
these last years of his life Wilkie Collins's works were written partly by others.   No evidence for this assertion has, as
yet, been revealed.   On the contrary, scholars find the works
to be consistent in style and content.   His surviving letters
to Watt indicate that Collins approached his works in the
1880's with the same diligence and meticulousness he had exhibited earlier in his life.

77.   In 1884 Collins sold a few stories; and the novel
"I Say No: or, The Love Letter Answered was published in
one volume by Harper and Brothers.   So eager were Harper
and Brothers and Collins to beat the pirates to press that the
American publisher, using manuscript instead of corrected
proofs, beat Chatto and Windus, the British publisher, to
publication by about four months.   The three-volume British
version was titled, simply, "I Say No".   The year was marred
by the death of Collins's close friend, Charles Reade.

78.   In 1885 a drama by Collins, The Evil Genius,
was produced for one performance at the Vaudeville Theatre
in October, for the securing of the copyright.   The play was
rewritten into narrative form and published in The Leigh
Journal and Times, part of a chain of newspapers owned by
Tillotson and Company of Bolton, from December 1885 into
May 1886.   Chatto and Windus brought out a three-volume
edition in 1886.   He earned more money from the novel Evil
Genius than from any other.

79.   In 1885 and 1886, Collins had short stories and
one nonfiction article published.   He wrote a novel, The
Guilty River, for Arrowsmith's Christmas Annual, a one-

volume book published by J. W. Arrowsmith of London in
1886.   Harper and Brothers published the novel as part of
the firm's Harper's Handy Series, also in 1886.

80.   Collins spent the early months of 1887 preparing
a collection of his stories, which was published in three volumes by Chatto and Windus, entitled Little Novels.   Harry
Quilter, a young critic, published an article, "A Living Story-
Teller," in the Contemporary Review, during this late period
of Collins's life.   In 1887, Collins, naturally enough, took a
liking to Quilter, who had praised Collins highly.   Critics,
long sour on Collins, were virtually ignoring him.   Quilter's
was the first in a series of critical works over several decades in which a critic tried to place Collins in his proper
critical and historical context.   Collins contributed a valuable
piece for future scholars when "How I Write My Books" was
published in The Globe.   The article describes the process
of writing The Woman in White.

81.   Wilkie Collins's health worsened in 1888.   "Reminiscences of a Story-Teller," was published by The Universal
Review from May to August 1888.   The article consists mostly of amusing anecdotes involving the reactions of people to
Collins's works.   The Legacy of Cain, the last novel written
fully by Collins, was serialized in the chain of newspapers
controlled by Tillotson and Company.   Chatto and Windus
brought out a three-volume edition of the novel in 1889.

82.   Once he completed The Legacy of Cain, Collins
began his last novel, Blind Love.   Shortly before the novel
began its run in The Illustrated London News, mid-summer
1889, Collins suffered an apparent stroke.   He had written
most of the novel, but was unable to finish it.   He asked
Walter Besant to complete the final portion of the book.
Besant consented, and found Collins's notes exceptionally
detailed.   Collins recovered for a time, then caught a res-
piratory disease.   He died on September 23, 1889.   Blind
Love was published in three volumes in 1890 by Chatto and
Windus.

INDEX TO THE ESSAY
(by Paragraph Number)

The Bibliography

Part I

EDITIONS OF COLLINS'S WORKS

BOOKS

1. COLLECTED WORKS

1   Wilkie Collins's Novels: A New Edition. 29 volumes.
London: Chatto and Windus, 1889-1908. (Also called:
Library Edition.) Includes:

2   After Dark (1902 and 1925). v + 392 pp. (Short
stories.)

3   Antonina: or, the Fall of Rome.
        1889: Piccadilly Novels. 420 pp.
        1897: 396 pp.
        1905: Library Edition. viii + 386 pp.
        1908: 396 pp.

4   Armadale (1895, 1903, 1908, and 1920). viii + 662 pp.

5   Basil (1894 and 1910). vii + 344 pp.
        Reprint of 1885 edition.
        Illustrated by John Gilbert and J. Mahoney.

6   The Black Robe (1897 and 1901). vii + 311 pp.

7   Blind Love (1891, 1907, and 1910).
        Preface by Walter Besant.
        Illustrated.
        Completed by Besant when Collins became ill.

8   The Dead Secret (1899, 1901, 1906, and 1929). x +
326 pp.
        In 1932 this version was published by both Chatto
and Windus and the Macmillan Company of Canada,
in Toronto.
        1932: New Piccadilly Library.

9   The Evil Genius: A Domestic Story (1892 and 1899).
viii + 312 pp.
        Reprint of 1887 edition.

10   The Fallen Leaves (1899). 355 pp.

11   The Frozen Deep and Other Tales (1892 and 1915).
        vi + 322 pp.
            Illustrated by George Du Maurier and J. Mahoney.
12   The Haunted Hotel: A Mystery of Modern Venice.
        My Lady's Money (1892 and 1902).   341 pp.
            Illustrated.
            In 1902, titled simply: The Haunted Hotel and My
        Lady's Money.
13   Heart and Science: A Story of the Present Time
        (1890, 1899, and 1913). x + 334 pp.
14   Hide and Seek.
15   "I Say No."   vii + 320 pp.
            1889: Piccadilly Novels.
            1894 and 1906: A new edition.
            Reprint of 1886 edition.
16   Jezebel's Daughter (1897? and 1901).   v + 330 pp.
17   The Law and the Lady: A Novel (1889, 1903, and
        1908).   viii + 429 pp.
            Reprint of 1885 edition.
18   The Legacy of Cain (1891, 1906?, 1915, and 1932).
        vi + 322 pp.
            1915: Khaki Library.
            In 1932 this version was published by both Chatto
        and Windus and the Macmillan Company of Canada,
        in Toronto.
            1932: New Piccadilly Library.
19   Little Novels (1889 and 1902).   318 pp.
20   Man and Wife: A Novel.
            1889: xii + 468 pp. (reprint of 1875 and 1887
        editions).
            1897, 1902, 1903, and 1907: xvi + 572 pp.
            In 1932 the 1889 version was published by both
        Chatto and Windus and the Macmillan Company of
        Canada, in Toronto.
            1932: New Piccadilly Library.
21   Miss or Mrs. ?: and Other Stories in Outline (1900
        and 1925).   vi + 298 pp.
22   The Moonstone: A Romance.
            1895 and 1897: 462 pp.
            1907: xii + 467 pp.
23   My Miscellanies (1898).   viii + 420 pp.
24   The New Magdalen: A Novel (1894 and 1925).   viii +
        403 pp.
            Illustrated by George Du Maurier and C. S. Rein-
        hart.
            Reprint of 1873 edition.
25   No Name (1904, 1921, 1928, and 1932).   548 pp.

In 1932 this version was published by both Chatto and Windus and the Macmillan Company of Canada, in Toronto.

1932: New Piccadilly Library.

26   Poor Miss Finch: A Domestic Story (1889 and 1913). viii + 432 pp.
27   The Queen of Hearts (1911). vii + 344 pp.
28   A Rogue's Life: From His Birth to His Marriage (1889, 1890, and 1903). iv + 188 pp.
29   The Two Destinies: A Romance (1906). viii + 341 pp.
30   The Woman in White.
        1890: Piccadilly Novels. viii + 494 pp. Reprint of 1875 edition. Illustrated by John Gilbert and F. A. Fraser.
        1896, 1906, 1928, and 1932: 565 pp.
        1932: New Piccadilly Library.

Chatto and Windus published other versions of these books. See BOOKS sections 2. and 4.a.

31   Wilkie Collins's Novels: Harper's Illustrated Library Edition. 17 volumes. New York and London: Harper and Brothers, 1873-1902. Includes:
32   After Dark: and Other Stories (1893 and 1899). 536 pp.
        Reprint of 1873 edition.
        Reprinted: Freeport, N. Y.: Books for Libraries Press, 1972. (Short Story Index Reprint Series.)
33   Antonina: or, The Fall of Rome (1893, 1898, 1904, and 1916). 438 pp.
34   Armadale: A Novel (1893, 1899, and 1902). 657 pp.
35   Basil: A Novel (1893, 1898, and 1904). vii + 336 pp.
36   The Dead Secret: A Novel (1893, 1899, and 1902). 359 pp.
37   Hide and Seek: or, The Mystery of Mary Grice: A Novel (1898 and 1904). 412 pp.
38   "I Say No": or, The Love Letter Answered: and Other Stories (1893, 1899, and 1916). 233 + 29 + 198 pp.
        Reprint of 1886 edition.
        Reprinted: Freeport, N. Y.: Books for Libraries Press, 1972. (Short Story Index Reprint Series.) (See entry 118.)
39   The Law and the Lady: A Novel (1899). 362 pp.
        Reprint of 1875 edition.
40   Man and Wife: A Novel (1893, 1899, 1902, 1911, and

1916).   562 pp.

41 The Moonstone: A Novel (1898, 1900, 1905, 1908,
    and ? 1924).   491 pp.
42 My Miscellanies (1893, 1899, 19--).   426 pp.
43 The New Magdalen (1902 and 1903).   325 pp.
44 No Name (1899 and 1911).   609 pp.
        Reprint of 1873 edition.
45 Poor Miss Finch: A Novel (1893, 1899, and 1902).
    454 pp.
        Reprint of 1873 edition.
        Reprinted: St. Clair Shores, Mich. : Scholarly
    Press, 1971, 1972.   (Literature Series.)
46 The Queen of Hearts: A Novel (1899 and 1902).   472 pp.
        In spite of the title, The Queen of Hearts is a col-
    lection of short stories (see section I. 4. b.)
47 The Two Destinies: A Novel (1893, 1899, and 1905).
    312 pp.
        Reprint of 1876 edition.
48 The Woman in White: A Novel (1893, 1899, 1900,
    1902) 548 pp.
        Reprint of 1873 edition.

49 The Works of Wilkie Collins.   30 volumes.   New York:
    Peter Fenelon Collier, 1900.   (Reprinted: New York:
    AMS Press, 1970).   Includes:
50   volume 1.   The Woman in White: A Novel (Part One).
        575 pp.
51   v. 2.   The Woman in White: A Novel (Part Two):
        Short Stories: The Dead Alive: The Fatal Cradle:
        Fatal Fortune: "Blow Up with the Brig!"   558 pp.
52   v. 3.   Man and Wife: A Novel (Part One).   577 pp.
53   v. 4.   Man and Wife: A Novel (Part Two): Short
        Stories: Miss or Mrs. ?: The Frozen Deep.   614 pp.
54   v. 5.   The Law and the Lady: A Novel.   559 pp.
55   v. 6.   The Moonstone (Part One).
56   v. 7.   The Moonstone (Part Two): The New Magdalen.
        602 pp.
57   v. 8.   Armadale (Part One).   579 pp.
58   v. 9.   Armadale (Part Two).   575 pp.
59   v. 10.   Basil: Little Novels: Mrs. Zant and the
        Ghost: Miss Morris and the Stranger: Mr. Lismore
        and the Widow.   579 pp.
60   v. 11.   Hide and Seek.   624 pp.
61   v. 12.   No Name (Part One).   576 pp.
62   v. 13.   No Name (Part Two): Little Novels: Mr.
        Cosway and the Landlady: Miss Mina and the Groom.
        576 pp.

| 63 | v. 14. | The Queen of Hearts: Little Novel: Mr. Lepel and the Housekeeper. 608 pp. |

63   v. 14.   The Queen of Hearts: Little Novel: Mr.
     Lepel and the Housekeeper. 608 pp.
64   v. 15.   Poor Miss Finch: A Domestic Story. 656
     pp.
65   v. 16.   The Dead Secret: A Novel: Little Novel:
     Miss Bertha and the Yankee. 590 pp.
66   v. 17.   Antonina: or, The Fall of Rome. 656 pp.
67   v. 18.   The Two Destinies: A Novel: Little Novels:
     Mr. Medhurst and the Princess: Miss Jeromette and
     the Clergyman: Mr. Captain and the Nymph: Mr.
     Marmaduke and the Minister: Mr. Percy and the
     Prophet. 575 pp.
68   v. 19.   After Dark. 544 pp.
69   v. 20.   My Miscellanies. 540 pp.
70   v. 21.   The Fallen Leaves. 525 pp.
71   v. 22.   The Haunted Hotel: A Mystery of Modern
     Venice: To Which Is Added: My Lady's Money. 477
     pp.
72   v. 23.   The Black Robe. 448 pp.
73   v. 24.   The Evil Genius: A Domestic Story. 464 pp.
74   v. 25.   Heart and Science: A Story of the Present
     Time. 539 pp.
75   v. 26.   The Legacy of Cain: A Novel. 480 pp.
76   v. 27.   Jezebel's Daughter. 416 pp.
77   v. 28.   Blind Love. 544 pp.
78   v. 29.   "I Say No." 512 pp.
79   v. 30.   A Rogue's Life: From His Birth to His
     Marriage: Little Novels: Miss Dulane and My Lord:
     Mr. Policeman and the Cook. 320 pp.

2.   NOVELS AND OTHER BOOK-LENGTH WORKS*

Antonina: or, The Fall of Rome. (1850.)

80   Antonina: or The Fall of Rome. London: Chatto and
     Windus, 1896. (Five Hundred Books Series.) New York:
     G. Routledge and Sons, 1897. 172 pp.

---

*Details on first editions and editions during Collins's life-
time are in the Bibliographic Essay (the index to which begins on page 22). The works in this section are in chronological order under each heading.

Armadale.   Serialized 1864-1866.   (1866.)

81 _____. New York: A. L. Burt, n. d.   (late 1890's).
676 pp.

82 _____. 2 volumes. New York: Street and Smith, n. d.

83 _____. London: Jarrolds, Publishers, 1923.   (Laurel
Library.)   384 pp.

84 _____. London and Dublin: Mellifont Press, 1947.
(Mellifont Classics, no. 43.)   285 pp.
Abridged.

85 _____. Toronto: Macmillan Company of Canada, 1932.
(New Piccadilly Library.)
See: Wilkie Collins's Novels: A New Edition (entry
1).

Basil: A Story of Modern Life.   (1852.)

86 Basil. New York: Federal Book Company, n. d.
(1890's).

87 _____. London: Downey, 1897. (6d. Library.) 386 pp.

88 _____. London: George Routledge and Sons, 1898.
(Handy Novels.)   274 pp.

89 _____. London: R. Butterworths, 1901.   256 pp.

Blind Love.   Serialized in 1889.   (1890.)

Collins's last illness interrupted his writing of
this novel.   At Collins's request, Walter Besant
finished it.   According to Besant, Collins's notes
were extraordinarily detailed, so that the finished
work's events were all Collins's.

90 _____. 2 volumes. Leipzig: Bernhard Tauchnitz,
1890. (Collection of British Authors. Tauchnitz Edition.
v. 2629-2630.)
Preface by Walter Besant.

91 Blind Love: A Novel. 3 volumes. London: Chatto
and Windus, 1890. Vol. I. xii + 304 pp., Vol. II.

viii + 304 pp., Vol. III.   viii + 316 pp.
Preface by Walter Besant.
Illustrated by A. Forester.

92   Blind Love.   New York: Daniel Appleton and Company,
1890.   (Appleton's Town and Country Library.)
Preface by Walter Besant.
Illustrated.

93   _____.   New York: Hurst and Company, n.d.

94   _____.   Chicago and New York: Rand, McNally and
Company, n.d.   (New Globe Library.)

95   _____.   Cleveland, Ohio: Arthur Westbrook Company,
n.d.   (Hart Series.)

The Dead Secret.
Serialized in 1857.   (1857.)

96   _____.   London: Chatto and Windus, 1899.   142 pp.

97   The Dead Secret: A Novel.   New York: Fifth Avenue
Publishing Company, 1900.   307 pp.
Illustrated.

98   The Dead Secret.   London: Downey, 1900.   316 pp.

99   _____.   London: Walter Scott Publishing Company,
1901.   (Oxford Library.)   404 pp.

100   _____.   New York: Street and Smith, 1901.

101   _____.   New York: Federal Book Company, n.d.
(1890's?).

102   _____.   New York: C. Scribner's Sons, 1908.   (Reprinted, 1909.)   x + 462 pp.
Illustrated by W. Sherman Potts.

103   _____.   New York: Dodd, Mead and Company, 1912.
543 pp.

104   _____.   London: Chapman and Dodd, Ltd., 1922.
(Abbey Library.)   317 pp.

105 _____ . New York: Street and Smith, n. d. (Select Library.)

106 _____ . London and Dublin: Mellifont Press, 1946. (Mellifont Classics.) 317 pp. Abridged.

The Evil Genius.
Serialized from 1885-1886. (1886.)

107 _____ . Chicago: M. A. Donohue and Company, n. d. (late 1890's or 1900).

108 _____ . New York: Federal Book Company, n. d. (1890's).

109 _____ . New York: Hurst and Company, n. d. (1890's). (Arlington Edition.)

110 _____ . New York: Street and Smith, 1901. (Arrow Library.)

111 _____ . New York: A. L. Burt and Company, n. d.

112 _____ . Cleveland, Ohio: Arthur Westbrook Company, n. d. (All Star Series.)

Heart and Science.
Serialized 1882-1883. (1883.)

113 _____ . Chicago: M. A. Donohue and Company, n. d. (probably in the 1900's).

Hide and Seek. (1854.)

114 Hide and Seek: A Novel. New York: Dick and Fitzgerald, 189-. 212 pp.

115 Hide and Seek: or, The Mystery of Mary Grice. London: George Routledge and Sons, 1898. (Handy Novels.) 372 pp.

116 _____ . London: R. Butterworth, 19--. 302 pp.

"I Say No": or The Love Letter
Answered.   (1884.)

117   _____.   New York: Street and Smith, 1902.   315 pp.

118   "I Say No": or, The Love-Letter Answered: and Other
Stories.   Freeport, N.Y.: Books for Libraries Press,
1972.   (Short Story Index Reprint Series.)   233 + 198
pp.
    Reprint of Harper and Brothers 1886 edition (see
entry 38).
    Contents: "'I Say No': or, The Love-Letter An-
swered," "The Ghost's Touch," "My Lady's Money: An
Episode in the Life of a Young Girl," "Percy and the
Prophet: Events in the Lives of a Lady and Her Lov-
ers. "

119   John Jasper's Secret: Sequel to Edwin Drood.   New
York: R. F. Fenno and Company, 1898.   (Reprinted,
1901.)   431 pp.
    First published in 1871.
    Reprinted in 1905, and entitled: John Jasper's Se-
cret: Sequel to Charles Dickens' Mystery of Edwin
Drood, by Henry Morford, formerly attributed to
Charles Dickens, the younger, and Wilkie Collins.
    The pre-1905 editions credited this book to Charles
Dickens, Jr. , and Wilkie Collins. Neither author had
anything to do with this work. Early bibliographies
tend to attribute this work to Collins, so scholars should
beware of it. Not Written by Wilkie Collins.

The Legacy of Cain.   (1888.)

120   _____.   3 volumes.   London: Chatto and Windus,
1889.   Vol. I.   viii + 289 pp. , Vol. II.   vi + 263 pp. ,
Vol. III.   vi + 281 pp.
    According to Michael Sadleir, this edition was ac-
tually published in 1888, in spite of its having been
dated 1889. See: Sadleir, "Wilkie Collins, 1824-1889"
(entry 434), page 150.

121   _____.   New York: National Publishing Company,
1891?.   301 pp.

122   _____.   New York: Federal Book Company, n. d.

123   _____.   Chicago: M. A. Donohue and Company, n. d.

Man and Wife.
First serialized 1869-1870.   (1870.)

124 _____ . New York: A. L. Burt, n. d.

125 _____ . 2 volumes. New York: Street and Smith, n. d.

Memoirs of the Life of
William Collins, Esq. , R. A.   (1848.)

126 Memoirs of the Life of William Collins, Esq. , R. A. :
With Selections from His Journals and Correspondence:
By His Son. 2 volumes. London: Longman, Brown,
Green, and Longmans, 1898.

The Moonstone.
Serialized in 1868.   (1868.)

See also: The Woman in White: and The Moonstone (entries 256 and 257).

127 _____ . New York: A. L. Burt Company, 189- (Burt's
Home Library).   19-- (Burt's Library of the World's
Best Books).   1908 (The Home Library.) 191- (Burt's
Home Library).   192- (Cornel Series) (The Home Li-
brary) (New Pocket Edition of Standard Classics).   1934
(Mammoth Series).   512 pp.

128 _____ . New York: R. F. Fenno and Company, 1900?.
409 pp.

129 _____ . Philadelphia: Henry T. Coates and Company,
n. d.

130 _____ . New York: H. M. Caldwell Company, n. d.

131 _____ . New York: American News Company, n. d.
(Favorite Library.)

132 The Moonstone: A Romance. London: Thomas Nelson
and Sons, 19--. 1925 (Nelson's Classics). 1930 (School
Classics).   1941 (Winchester Classics).   1954 (Nelson
Classic).   457 pp.

133 _____ . New York: L. Macveagh, Dial Press, 19--.
(Reprinted, 1925, Dial Press.) 500 pp.

134 The Moonstone. New York: Street and Smith, n. d.

135 _____ . Philadelphia: John C. Winston Company, n. d.

136 _____ . New York: Century Company, 1903. (English Comédie Humaine.) (Reprinted, 1904 and 1906.) 515 pp.

137 The Moonstone: A Romance. New York: C. Scribner's Sons, 1908. xii + 653 pp.
       Illustrated by John Sloan.

138 The Moonstone. New York: Hurst and Company, 1908.

139 _____ . London: W. Collins Sons and Company, 1910. (Illustrated Pocket Classics.) London and Glasgow: Collins' Clear-Type Press, 192-. London and New York: William Collins Sons and Company, 1930. 1932 (Canterbury Classics). 1937 (Collins' Illustrated Pocket Classics). 664 pp.
       Illustrated by A. Pearse.

140 _____ . 2 volumes. New York: Dodd, Mead and Company, 1912.

141 The Moonstone: A Romance. London: Herbert Jenkins, 1920. 381 pp.

142 The Moonstone. Garden City, New York: Garden City Publishing Company, 192-. (Sun Dial Press.)

143 The Moonstone: A Romance. London: George G. Harrap and Company, 1925. (Harrap's Standard Fiction Library.) 500 pp.

144 The Moonstone. New York: Dodd, Mead and Company, 1926. (Astor Library.) 500 pp.

145 _____ . London: Oxford University Press, 1928. (The World's Classics.) (Reprinted, 1932, 1934, 1945, 1949, 1951, and 1966.) xx + 522 pp.
       Introduction by T. S. Eliot.
       T. S. Eliot's introduction is based on an essay first printed in the Times Literary Supplement in 1927 (see entry 541), which has been reprinted in Eliot's Selected Essays, 1917-1932 (see entry 443) and elsewhere (also see entry 443).
       This edition of The Moonstone is frequently referred to by scholars and critics.

146   "The Moonstone. " Condensed by Jessie A. Parsons.
One Hundred World's Best Novels Condensed. Ed. Edwin
A. Grozier.   Assisted by Charles E. L. Wingate and
Charles H. Lincoln.   New York: Blue Ribbon Books, Inc. ,
1931.   Pp. 497-500 (total book length: viii + 535
pp).
This anthology includes "The Woman in White" (entry
225).
A brief plot summary.

147   The Moonstone.   Glasgow: Blackie and Son, 1931.
(Great Novelists Library.)   xi + 464 pp.
Illustrated.

148   _____ .   New York: Harper and Brothers, 1931.   (Harper Sealed Mystery Story.)   482 pp.
Pages 313-482 sealed (entire edition) as an added
feature to emphasize the suspense of the story.

149   _____ .   London: Chatto and Windus, 1932.   Toronto:
Macmillan Company of Canada, 1932.   (New Piccadilly
Library.)   458 pp.

150   _____ .   London: Jonathan Cape, Ltd. , 1933.   Toronto,
Canada: Thomas Nelson and Sons, 1933.   (Florin
Books.)   448 pp.

151   _____ .   London: Queensway Press, 1935.   381 pp.
Abridged.

152   _____ .   Abridged and Edited by Bhupal Singh.   London:
Oxford University Press, 1935.   (Herbert Strang's Li-
brary.)   338 pp.
Abridged.

153   _____ .   London: Virtue and Company, n. d. (probably
the 1930's).

154   _____ .   New York: Editions for the Armed Services,
194-.   (Armed Services Edition.)   511 pp.

155   _____ .   New York: Books, Inc. , 1944.   (Duo-Tone
Classics.)   (Registered Guild Club.)   389 pp.

156   _____ .   New York: The Press of the Readers Club,
1943.   xiv + 472 pp.
Foreword by Alexander Woollcott.

Reviewed in New York Herald-Tribune Book Review (entry 627).

157 _____. Garden City, N. Y. : Doubleday, Doran and Company, 1944. Toronto, Canada: McClelland and Stewart, Ltd. , 1944. (Reprinted by both publishers, 1946 (Doubleday Illustrated Classics).) 444 pp.
Illustrated by William Sharp.
Reprinted: Garden City, N. Y. : Garden City Publishing Company, 1948.

158 The Moonstone: Adapted and Simplified. Ed. Evelyn May Attwood. London: Longmans Green and Company, 1950. (Longmans Simplified English Series.) ix + 147 pp.
Illustrated.

159 The Moonstone. New York: Almat Publishing Corporation, 1950. (Pyramid Books, 19.) 320 pp.

160 The Moonstone: with Lithographs in Full Color. New York: Phillip C. Duschnes, 1951. London: Cassell and Company, 1951 (Folio Society). 417 pp.
Lithographs by Edwin La Dell.

161 The Moonstone. Ed. G. D. H. Cole and Margaret Cole. London and Toronto: William Collins Sons and Company, 1953 (Collins New Classics). 1956 (New School Classics). 448 pp. Bibliography: pp. 447-448.
Reprinted: New York: W. W. Norton and Company, 1959.
Reprinted: London and Glasgow: William Collins Sons and Company, 1965.

162 _____. London: University of London Press, 1954. Reprinted: 1955. (Pilot Books) 192 pp.
Illustrated.

163 _____. Harmondsworth, Middlesex, England: Penguin Books, 1955. (Penguin Books, no. 1072.) 464 pp.

164 The Moonstone: With Illustrations of the Author and the Setting of the Book Together with an Introduction and Descriptive Captions. New York: Dodd, Mead and Company, 1955. (Great Illustrated Classics.) 444 pp.
Introduction and captions by Basil Davenport.
Illustrated by William Sharp.

The introduction is a brief biographical sketch of Collins.

165   The Moonstone: Abridged and Adapted.   Ed.   E.   F. Dodd.   New York: Macmillan, 1956.   (Illustrated Stories to Remember Series.)   164 pp.

166   The Moonstone.   London: Longmans Green and Company, 1956.   448 pp.

167   _____.   New York: E. P. Dutton and Company, 1944. London: J. M. Dent and Sons, Ltd. , 1944.   (Reprinted, 1945, 1957, 1962.)   (Everyman's Library, no.   979.) xviii + 430 pp.   "Bibliographical Note":   page xiii.
Introduction by Dorothy Sayers.
The introduction is often referred to by scholars and critics.
Reviewed in College English (entry 628).

168   _____.   New York: For the members of the Limited Editions Club, 1959.   New York: Heritage Press, 1960. xviii + 464 pp.
Introduction by Vincent Starrett.
Illustrated by Andres Dignimont.

169   _____.   New York: Doubleday and Company, 1960. London: Mayflower Books, Ltd. , 1960.   (Dolphin Book.)   520 pp.

170   _____.   Abridged by Oswald Harland.   Huddersfield: Schofield and Sims Ltd. , 1961.   (Shortened Classics.) 298 pp.

171   _____.   Glasgow: Blackie and Son, Ltd. , 1961. (Chosen Books no.   61.)   448 pp.
Illustrated by Peter Edwards.

172   _____.   Abridged by Anthea Beamish.   London: Longmans Green and Company, 1961.   (Longmans' Abridged Books)   xi + 284 pp.
Introduction by Anthea Beamish.

173   _____.   Abridged by Anthea Beamish.   London: Longmans Green and Company, 1962.   (Longmans' Abridged Books.)   xi + 260 pp.
Introduction by Anthea Beamish.

174   _____.   Abridged by Ruth Gillham.   London: Oxford

University Press, 1963. (English-Reader's Library.)
viii + 183 pp.
   Illustrated by Lynton Lamb.

175 _____. Ed. Maurice Walton Thomas and Gladys Thomas.
London and Boston: Ginn and Company, 1966. (Shorter
Classics.) x + 182 pp.
   Illustrated by John Sergeant.

176 _____. New York: Harper and Row, Publishers,
1965. (A "Perennial Classic. ") xvii + 462 pp. Bibliography: page x.

177 _____. Ed. J. I. M. Stewart. Harmondsworth, Middlesex, England: Penguin Books, 1966. (Reprinted:
1969, 1971, 1973.) (Penguin English Library.) 528 pp.
   Introduction by J. I. M. Stewart.
   "A Note on Sources" (Collins's sources for The
Moonstone): pp. 527-528.
   Stewart's introduction is thorough and useful. He
suggests that Coleridge might have added The Moonstone
to his last of the three most perfectly plotted works in
literature--Oedipus Tyrannus by Sophocles, The Alchemist
by Ben Jonson, and Tom Jones by Henry Fielding.
Stewart evaluates The Moonstone and provides some
biographical and scholarly information.

178 _____. London: Pan Books, 1967. (Panbooks no.
T30. One of the Bestsellers of Literature.) 494 pp.
Bibliography: pages 493-494.
   Introduction by Anthony Burgess.
   Notes by David Williams.

179 The Moonstone: Large Type Edition: Complete and
Unabridged. New York: Franklin Watts, Inc. , 1967.
(Keith Jennison Large Type Books.) viii + 804 pp.

180 The Moonstone. Abridged and adapted by Carli Laklan.
Palo Alto, Calif. : Fearon Publishers, Inc. , 1967.
(Pacemaker Classics.) 91 pp.
   Illustrated by Meredith Brooks.

181 _____. London: Heron Books, 1969. vi + 430 pp.
   Introduction by Malcolm Elwin.
   Illustrated by Charles Keeping.

182 _____. New York: Airmont, 1975?. (Classics Series.)

183   _____ . Rivercity Press, 1976.
        Reprint of 1868 edition.

184   The Moonstone: and The Woman in White. New York:
      Random House, 1937 (Modern Library of World's Best
      Books). (Reprinted, 1941.) London: Hamish Hamil-
      ton, 1937 (Modern Library Giants). Toronto: Macmil-
      lan Company of Canada, 1937 (Modern Library Giants).
      viii + 843 pp.
        Foreword by Alexander Woollcott.
        Reprinted: New York: Modern Library, 1964. (Mod-
      ern Library of the World's Best Books.)

                    The New Magdalen.
              Serialized in 1872.   (1873.)

185   _____ . New York: International Book Company, 189-.
      (New Columbus Series.) 206 pp.

186   The New Magdalen: A Novel. London: Chatto and
      Windus, 1900.   126 pp.

187   The New Magdalen. Chicago: M. A. Donohue and
      Company, n. d.

188   _____ . New York: American News Company, n. d.
      (Favorite Library.)

189   _____ . New York: Street and Smith, 1900.   (Arrow
      Library.)

190   _____ . New York: C. Scribner's Sons, 1908.   ix +
      366 pp.
        Illustrated by John Sloan.

191   _____ . New York: A. L. Burt and Company, n. d.

            No Name.   Serialized 1862-1863.   (1862.)

192   _____ . New York: A. L. Burt and Company, 1899?.

193   _____ . London: William Collins Sons and Company,
      1905.   (Handy Pocket Novels.) (Reprinted, 192-; Col-
      lins' Illustrated Pocket Classics.)   680 pp.
        Illustrated.

194 _____ . London: William Collins Sons and Company, 1905.

195 _____ . Philadelphia: John C. Winston Company, 1907.

196 _____ . Ed. Herbert van Thal. New York: Stein and Day, 1967. London: Anthony Blond, Ltd. , 1967. (Doughty Library, no. 2.) 593 pp.
Introduction by Herbert van Thal.
No Name is one of a series of books edited by Herbert van Thal for the Doughty Library.
Reviewed by Peter Caracciolo, K. T. Willis, Michael Thorpe, and John Goode, and in the Times Literary Supplement (entries 629, 633, 632, 631, 630).

Poor Miss Finch.
Serialized 1871-1872.   (1872.)

197 Poor Miss Finch: A Domestic Story. New York: C. Scribner's Sons, 1908. xii + 552 pp.
Illustrated by Rollin C. Kirby.

Rambles Beyond Railways: or, Notes
in Cornwall Taken A-Foot.   (1851.)

198 _____ . London: Westaway Books Limited, 1948. x + 195 pp.
Introduction by Ashley Rowe.
Includes: "The Cruise of the Tomtit to the Scilly Islands, " pp. 165-195.
Reprint of 1851 edition.

The Woman in White.
Serialized 1859-1860.   (1860.)

See also: The Moonstone: and The Woman in White (entry 184).

199 _____ . New York: A. L. Burt, 189-. (Reprinted, 1907 (The Home Library).) (Reprinted: 1926.)   616 pp.

200 _____ . London: Chatto and Windus, 1894. (Reprinted, 1895.) vi + 238 pp.

201   The Woman in White: A Novel. New York and London:
      G. P. Putnam's Son, 19--. (Library of Famous Novels.)
      (Reprinted, 1917.) 682 pp.

202   The Woman in White. New York: Cassell and Company,
      1902. (Cassell's Standard Library.) 427 pp.

203   _____. London: Chatto and Windus, 1902. (St. Mar-
      tin's Library.) ix + 642 pp.

204   _____. Chicago: Laird and Lee, n. d. (Pastime
      Series.)

205   _____. Philadelphia: Henry T. Coates and Company,
      19-- (1900?). 616 pp.

206   _____. New York: Federal Book Company, n. d.

207   _____. New York: George W. Dillingham Company,
      n. d.

208   _____. Ed. Hannaford Bennett. London: Long, 1903.
      (Long's Library of Modern Classics.) xvi + 573 pp.
      Introduction by Hannaford Bennett.
      Illustrated by A. T. Smith.

209   _____. London: James Nisbet and Company, 1904.

210   _____. London: George Routledge and Sons, 1904.

211   _____. London: William Collins Sons and Company,
      1904 (Handy Illustrated Pocket Novels). 1914 and 192-?
      (Collins's Illustrated Pocket Classics, 18). 1930 (Can-
      terbury Classics). 614 pp.
      Illustrated by T. Eyre Macklin.

212   _____. London: William Collins Sons and Company,
      1905.

213   _____. New York: Century Company, 1906. (English
      Comédie Humaine, 2nd Series.) vii + 584 pp.
      Illustrated.

214   _____. London: L. Collins, 1906. (Home Library.)
      518 pp.

215   _____. London: John Long and Company, 1908.

216 _____ . London: Cassell and Company, 1908.
(People's Library, vol. 59.) 535 pp.

217 _____ . 2 volumes. New York: C. Scribner's Sons,
1908. (Reprinted, 1909.)
     Illustrated by W. Sherman Potts.

218 _____ . New York: E. P. Dutton and Company, 1910.
London: J. M. Dent and Sons, 1910. (Everyman's
Library.) (Reprinted, 1913, 1917, 1932, 1955, 1956,
1962, 1963.) xii + 570 pp.
     Introduction to 1910 through 1932 editions by Ernest
Rhys.
     Introduction to 1955 and after editions by Maurice
Richardson.

219 _____ . London: Thomas Nelson and Sons, 1910 (Nelson's Classics). (Reprinted: 1922 (Nelson's Classics)
and 1935 (Winchester Classics).) 572 pp.

220 _____ . London: Ward, Lock and Company, 1911.
(World Library.) 574 pp.

221 _____ . 2 volumes. New York: Dodd, Mead and
Company, 1912.

222 _____ . New York: Hurst and Company, n. d.

223 _____ . Philadelphia: John C. Winston Company,
n. d.

224 _____ . London: "Weekly Telegraph, " 1916.   94 pp.

225 "The Woman in White. " Condensed by Alice Fox Pitts.
One Hundred World's Best Novels Condensed.   Ed.
Edwin A. Grozier. Assisted by Charles E. L. Wingate
and Charles H. Lincoln. New York: Blue Ribbon
Books, Inc. , 1931. Pp. 354-357 (total book length:
viii + 535 pp.).
     This anthology includes "The Moonstone" (entry 146).
A brief plot summary.

226 _____ . London: Oxford University Press, 1922.
(World's Classics, no. 226.) (Reprinted, 1926, 1932,
1933, 1949.) vii + 636 pp.

227 _____ . London: Robert Hayes, Ltd. , 1925. (Sand-
ringham Library.) 377 pp.

228 _____ . London: Readers' Library Publishing Company,
1927. (Readers' Library.) 253 pp.

229 The Woman in White: Suitably Abridged.   London: D.
C. Thomson and Company, 1927. (Red Letter Novels,
no. 183.) 160 pp.

230 The Woman in White.   New York: Funk and Wagnalls
Company, n. d.   (People's Library.)

231 _____ . Glasgow: Blackie and Son, 1931. (Reprinted:
1932.) (Great Novelists Library.) vi + 574 pp.
Illustrated.

232 _____ . New York and London: Harper and Brothers,
1932. (Harper Sealed Mystery.) 530 pp.
Pages 313 through 530 sealed (entire edition) as an
added feature to emphasize the suspense of the story.
Slightly abridged.

233 _____ . Chicago: Consolidated Book Publishers, Inc. ,
1937. (Classic Romances of Literature, vol. 4.)
Reading, Pennsylvania: Spencer Press, 1937. viii + 630
pp.

234 The Woman in White: Abridged and Simplified.   Ed.
L. R. H. Chapman and L. Robinson.   London: University of London Press, 1937. (Pilot Books for Boys
and Girls Series.) viii + 200 pp.
Illustrated by Lorna R. Steele.

235 The Woman in White.   15 volumes.   Cleveland, Ohio:
Cleveland Chapter of the American Red Cross, 1942.
Braille 1 1/2.

236 "The Woman in White. " Novels of Mystery from the
Victorian Age: Four Complete Novels.   Ed. Maurice
Lane Richardson.   London: Pilot Press, 1945.   New
York: Duell, 1947. xviii + 678 pp.
Introduction by Maurice Richardson.
Includes: Carmilla by J. Sheridan LeFanu; Dr. Jekyll
and Mr. Hyde by R. L. Stevenson; and Notting Hill
Mystery by an anonymous writer.
Reviewed by John Farrelly and in the Times Literary
Supplement (see entries 635 and 636).

237 The Woman in White.   London: Mellifont Press, 1946.

(Mellifont Classics, no. 27.)   285 pp.
    Abridged.

238   _____ .   Cleveland and New York: World Publishing
Company, 1947.   Toronto, Canada: McClelland and
Stewart, 1947.   630 pp.
    Illustrated.

239   _____ .   London: Dymock's Book Arcade, Ltd., 1947.
(Kingston Classics.)   600 pp.

240   _____ .   London: Todd Publishing Company, 1948.
Toronto, Canada: Clarke, Irwin and Company, 1948.
(Modern Reading Library.)   160 pp.

241   _____ .   London and Glasgow: William Collins Sons
and Company, 1954.   (Reprinted: New York: W. W.
Norton and Company, and London: William Collins
Sons and Company, 1959 and 1966.)   573 pp.   Biblio-
graphy.
    Introduction by E. C. R. Lorac (pseudonym for
Edith Caroline Rivett).

242   The Woman in White: Shortened and Simplified.   Ed.
G. C. Thornley.   London: Longmans Green and Company, 1954.   (Longmans Simplified English Series.)
vii + 119 pp.
    Illustrated by Rosemary Brown.

243   The Woman in White.   London: Thomas Nelson and
Sons, 1954.   (Nelson Classics.)   xiii + 674 pp.

244   _____ .   New York: Phillip C. Duschnes, 1956.   London: Folio Society, 1956.   540 pp.
    Lithographs by Lynton Lamb.

245   _____ .   New York: Doubleday and Company, 1961.
(Dolphin Books.)   555 pp.

246   _____ .   Ed. Maurice Walton Thomas and Gladys Thomas.   London and Boston: Ginn and Company, 1962.
(Shorter Classics.)   x + 182 pp.
    Illustrated by Patrick Stackhouse.

247   _____ .   New York: Heritage Press, 1964.   Woodstock,
Vt.:   Printed for the Members of the Limited Editions
Club at the Elm Tree Press, 1964.   xvi + 534 pp.

Introduction by Vincent Starrett.
Illustrated by Leonard Rosoman.
Starrett refers to The Woman in White as "auto-
biographic writing" on page vii.

248 _____ . New York: Popular Library, Inc. , 1964.
589 pp.

249 _____ . New York: Paperback Library, 1966.   (A
Paperback Library Gothic.)   352 pp.
Abridged.

250 _____ . London: Heron Books, 1969.   (Literary Heri-
tage Collection.)   571 pp.
Introduction by E. C. R. Lorac (pseudonym for
Edith Caroline Rivett).

251 _____ . Ed. Anthea Trodd.   Boston: Houghton Mifflin
Company, 1969.   (Riverside Editions.)   xxx + 514 pp.
Introduction by Kathleen Tillotson, "The Lighter
Reading of the Eighteen-Sixties. "   pp. ix-xxvi.
"A Note on the Text": Anthea Trodd, pp. xxvii-
xxviii.
Preface by Gordon N. Ray, pp. v-vi.
"Appendix A: Prefaces to the Editions of 1860 and
1861, " pp. 499-502.
"Appendix B: Review, 'The Woman in White,' The
Times, 30 October 1860, " pp. 503-510.
"Appendix C: Wilkie Collins, 'How I Write My
Books,'" The Globe, 26 November 1887, " pp. 511-514.
Kathleen Tillotson discusses the "sensation novel"
in general.   "How I Write My Books" is Collins's de-
scription of the writing of The Woman in White.

252 _____ . New York: Popular Library Publishers, 1970.
589 pp.

253 _____ . Ed. Julian Symons.   London: Penguin Books,
1974.   (Penguin English Library.)   648 pp.
Introduction by Julian Symons.

254 _____ . Ed. Harvey Peter Sucksmith.   London: Oxford University Press, 1975.   xxxviii + 624 pp.
Introduction by Harvey Peter Sucksmith.

255 _____ . Rivercity, Mass. : Rivercity Press, 1976.
(American Reprints.)

Reprint of 1860 edition.

256 The Woman in White: and The Moonstone. London:
Chatto and Windus, 1896. 428 pp.

257 _____. Adapted by Verda Evans. New York: Globe
Book Company, 1953. (The Woman in White, 223 pp. ;
The Moonstone, 229 pp.)
Illustrated.

3. PLAYS

258 Black and White. First performed at the Adelphi
Theatre in 1869. First printed in 1869.
This play was written by Collins and Charles Fech-
ter in collaboration.

259 Black and White: A Drama in Three Acts. Chicago:
Dramatic Publishing Company, n. d. (about 1900). 34
pp.
This is probably based on the edition published by
Robert M. De Witt of New York in the 1870's (?).

260 The Frozen Deep: A Drama. First performed at
Charles Dickens's Tavistock House in 1857. Revised
and printed in 1866.

261 Under the Management of Charles Dickens: His Production of "The Frozen Deep. " Ed. Robert Louis
Brannan. Ithaca, N. Y. : Cornell University Press,
1966. xi + 173 pp. Bibliography: pp. 161-173.
Introduction by Robert Louis Brannan, pp. 1-90.
Based on Brannan's dissertation, The Frozen Deep:
Under the Management of Mr. Charles Dickens (entry
361).
According to Brannan, "The reviewers judged the
performances to be superior to anything on the professional stage; some thought the acting, especially Dickens', so unusual that its example might revolutionize
the professional theatre" (about the 1857 performance,
on page 1). Brannan uses extensive scholarship to
support the following point: "Indeed Dickens was also
a principal author of the script" (page 1).
A good piece of scholarship, Brannan's introduction

and text are informative and valuable.
Reviewed by Harvey C. Gardner, Phillip Collins, John W. Robinson, Leslie C. Staples, and in <u>Choice</u> (see entries 624, 623, 625, 626, 622).

262 <u>No Name: A Drama, in Four Acts</u>. Originally written in five acts in 1863. Published in four acts in 1870.

263 <u>No Name: A Drama in Five Acts</u>. Adapted by William Bayle Bernard. Chicago: Dramatic Publishing Company, 189-. (World Acting Drama.) 39 pp.
This play was adapted from Collins's novel, <u>No Name</u>.

264 <u>No Thoroughfare: A Drama: In Five Acts</u>. First performed at the Adelphi Theatre in December 1867. First printed in 1867.

265 <u>No Thoroughfare: A Drama</u>. Chicago: Dramatic Publishing Company, n.d. (1900's?).
Although this edition credits Charles Dickens with authorship--probably because Collins and Dickens collaborated on the fictional version published in <u>All the Year Round</u>--Collins is the sole author of the play.

4.   SHORT WORKS AND CORRESPONDENCE

a.   BOOKS DEVOTED SOLELY TO COLLINS*

<u>After Dark</u>.   (1856.)
<u>Short story</u> collection.

Contents: "Leaves from Leah's Diary" (used as a narrative connection between the short stories). "The Traveller's Story of a Terribly Strange Bed" (1852). "The Lawyer's Story of a Stolen Letter" (1854). "The French Governess's Story of Sister Rose" (1855). "The Angler's Story of the Lady of Glenwith Grange" (1856). "The Nun's Story of

*Details on first editions and editions during Collins's lifetime are in the Bibliographic Essay (the index to which begins on page 22). The works in this section are in chronological order under each heading.

Gabriel's Marriage" (1853).   "The Professor's
Story of the Yellow Mask" (1855).   "Last Leaves
from Leah's Diary. "

266   _____ . London: Gresham Publishing Company, 1900.
(Reprinted, 1924.) xx + 355 pp.
   Introduction by W. A. Brockington (biographical).
   Illustrated by Gordon Browne.
   Reprinted: Glasgow: Blackie and Son, 1904.   ix +
355 pp. (This reprint lacks the introduction.)

267   _____ . New York: Dodd, Mead and Company, 1912.
544 pp.
   Illustrated.

268   _____ . Glasgow: Blackie and Son, Ltd. , 1934. (Great
Novelists' Library.) vi + 320 pp.
   Illustrated by Gordon Browne.

269   After Dark: and Other Stories.   Freeport, N. Y. : Books
for Libraries Press, 1972.   (Short Story Index Reprint
Series.) 536 pp.
   Reprint of Harper and Brothers's 1875 edition.
   In addition to the complete text of After Dark, this
edition contains: "Miss or Mrs. ?" (1871), "The Dead
Alive" (1873-1874), "The Fatal Cradle, Otherwise, the
Heart Rending Story of Mr. Heavysides" (1861), "The
Frozen Deep" (the narrative version) (1874), "Fatal
Fortune" (1874).

270   The Best of Wilkie Collins.   Ed. George Bisserov.
New York: Juniper Press, 1959. (Forgotten Classics
of Mystery, vol. 1.) 383 pp.

"The Biter Bit. " First published
as "Who Is the Thief?" (1858).

271   The Biter Bit: The Black Cottage.   London: Holerth
Press, 1924. (Holerth Library, no. 48.) 60 pp.
   "The Black Cottage" was first published in 1857,
under the title "The Seige of the Black Cottage. " Both
stories were published in The Queen of Hearts (1859).
(See section I. 4. a.)

272   Matthew Sharpin, Detective: Originally Published Under
the Title The Biter Bit.   London: Todd Publishing
Company, 1943. (Polybooks.) 16 pp.

"The Dream Woman. "
First published in 1855 as "The Ostler. "

273   The Dream Woman.   Girard, Kan. : Haldeman-Julius
Company, 1923.   (Little Blue Book No. 107.)   96 pp.
Bibliography: page 94.
     Contents: "The Dream Woman, " "The Yellow Tiger"
(1857).

The Frozen Deep and Other Stories.   (1874.)
Also known as Readings and Writings in America:
The Frozen Deep and Other Stories.

Contents: "The Frozen Deep" (the narrative version) (1874), "The Dream Woman" (1855), "John
Jago's Ghost or The Dead Alive" (1873-1874) (the
same story as "The Dead Alive").

274   The Frozen Deep: and Other Tales.   London: Chatto
and Windus, 1904.   288 pp.
     Contents are as above.

"The Ghost's Touch. "   (1879.)

275   The Ghost's Touch: A Novel.   Springfield, Mass. :
Springfield Publishing Company, 1893.   (Advance Library, no. 83.)   125 pp.
     "The Ghost's Touch" is what was called a "little
novel"--a novelette.

"The Girl at the Gate. "   (1884.)

276   The Girl at the Gate.   New York: George Munro's
Sons, n. d. (pre-1900?).

The Guilty River.   (1886.)

277   _____ .   Bristol: J. W. Arrowsmith Ltd. , 1899.   (Reprinted, 1911.)   188 pp.

278   _____ .   Chicago: W. B. Conkey Company, n. d.
(1900's).

The Haunted Hotel. (1878.)

279 _____. New York: George Munro's Sons, n. d. (pre-
1900?).

280 _____. London: Chatto and Windus, 1909.

"How I Write My Books. " (1887.)

281/2 "How I Write My Books: Related in a Letter to a
Friend. " The Woman in White, ed. Anthea Trodd.
Boston: Houghton Mifflin Company, 1969. "Appendix
C, " pp. 511-514.
    See entry 251 for more information.

I Say No: or, The Loveletter
Answered: and Other Stories.

See section I. 2.

"The Lady of Glenwith Grange. "

First published in 1856 in After Dark and titled
"The Angler's Story of the Lady of Glenwith
Grange. "

283 _____. Eyre and Spottiswoode (Publishers) Ltd. , 1947.
(Atlantis Press Book.) 54 pp.

"Love's Random Shot. " (1884.)

284 Love's Random Shot: and Other Stories. New York:
George Munro's Sons, Publishers, 1894. 96 pp.
    Contents: "Love's Random Shot, " "The Dream
Woman" (1855).

285 Love's Random Shot. New York: F. Tennyson Neely,
n. d. (1890's).

286 _____. New York: Abbey Press, n. d. (1890's).

287 _____. New York: Hurst and Company, n. d. (1890's).

Matthew Sharpin, Detective: Originally
Published Under the Title The Biter Bit.

See under "The Biter Bit. "

"Miss or Mrs. ?"   (1871.)

288   Miss or Mrs. ? New York: E. Brandus and Company,
1891. (Mayfair Series, no. 3.) 172 pp.
In addition to "Miss or Mrs. ?" this book contains
"Blow Up with the Brig!" (1859).

289   Miss or Mrs. New York: J. S. Ogilvie Publishing
Company, n. d. (1890's).

290   Miss or Mrs. : or The Clandestine Marriage. New
York, 1903. 16 pp.

"My Lady's Money. "   (1877.)

291   My Lady's Money. New York: Street and Smith, 1898.
(Arrow Library, no. 58.) 174 pp.

292   _____ . London: Holerth Press, 1924. (Holerth Library.) 168 pp.

My Miscellanies.   (1863.)

Contents: "Talk-Stoppers" (1856). "A Journey in
Search of Nothing" (1857). "A Queen's Revenge"
(1857). "A Petition to the Novel-Writers" (1856).
"Laid Up in Lodgings" (1856). "A Shockingly Rude
Article" (1858). "The Great (Forgotten) Invasion"
(1859). "The Unknown Public" (1858). "Give Us
Room!" (1858). "Portrait of an Author, Painted
by His Publisher" (1859). "My Black Mirror"
(1856). "Mrs. Badgery" (1857). "Memoirs of
an Adopted Son" (1861). "The Bachelor Bedroom"
(1859). "A Remarkable Revolution" (1857).
"Douglas Jerrold" (1859). "Pray Employ Major
Namby!" (1859). "The Poisoned Meal" (1858).
"My Spinsters" (1856). "Dramatic Grub Street
(Explored in Two Letters)" (1858). "To Think,
or Be Thought For?" (1856). "Save Me from My

55   Short Works

Friends" (1858).   "The Cauldron of Oil" (1861).
"Bold Words by a Bachelor" (1856).   "Mrs. Bull-
winkle" (1858).   All of the articles were published
either in Household Words or All the Year Round.

293   _____. Westmead, Farnborough, Hants., England:
Gregg International Publishers, 1971. viii + 420 pp.
   Illustrated by Alfred Concanen.
   Reprint of 1875 Chatto and Windus edition.
   This edition contains all the works listed in entry
except "Dramatic Grub Street (Explored in Two Letters)"
is omitted.   In addition, the other articles are
rearranged.

   "Percy and the Prophet."   First published
   in 1877 as "Mr. Percy and the Prophet."

294   Percy and the Prophet.   London: Holerth Press, 1924.
(Holerth Library, vol. 56.)   80 pp.

295   Percy and the Prophet: and Ghost's Touch.   New York:
George Munro's Sons, n.d. (1890's?).
   "The Ghost's Touch" was first published in 1879.

   The Queen of Hearts.   (1859.)
   Short story collection.

Contents: "The Queen of Hearts" (provides the con-
necting narrative for the other stories).   "Brother
Owen's Story of the Black Cottage" (1857). "Brother
Griffith's Story of the Family Secret" (1857).
"Brother Morgan's Story of the Dream Woman"
(1855).   "Brother Griffith's Story of Mad Monkton"
(1855).   "Brother Morgan's Story of the Dead
Hand" (1857).   "Brother Griffith's Story of the
Biter Bit" (1858).   "Brother Owen's Story of the
Parson's Scruple" (1859).   "Brother Griffith's
Story of a Plot in Private Life" (1858).   "Brother
Morgan's Story of Fauntleroy" (1858).   "Brother
Owen's Story of Anne Rodway" (1856).

296   _____. New York: Street and Smith, 1900. (Arrow
Library.)

297   _____. New York: Arno, 1976. (Literature of Mystery and Detection.)

"A Rogue's Life. "   (1856.)

298   A Rogue's Life.   New York: George Munro's Sons,
      1890.   (Crescent Edition.)   (Seaside Library Pocket
      Edition.)   188 pp.

299   A Rogue's Life: From His Birth to His Marriage.   New
      York: F. M. Lupton Publishing Company, 189-.
      (Stratford Edition.)   204 pp.

300   _____.   New York: Optimus Printing Company, 189-.
      204 pp.

301   A Rogue's Life.   New York: Lupton, 1893.   (Armchair
      Library.)   61 pp.

302   _____.   New York: Federal Book Company, n. d.
      (1890's).

303   _____.   New York: Hurst and Company, n. d. (1890's).

304   A Rogue's Life: Written by Himself.   London and New
      York: Unit Library Ltd. , 1903.   (Unit Library, no.
      29.)   140 pp.

305   A Rogue's Life.   New York: J. S. Ogilvie Publishing
      Company, 1906.   (Sunset Series.)

306   _____.   London: Holden and Hardingham, Ltd. , 1915.

307   _____.   New York: Greenberg, Publisher, Inc. , 1926.
      (Rogues Bookshelf.)
      Introduction by Frank W. Chandler.

308   Short Stories of Wilkie Collins.   Selected by J. I. Ro-
      dale.   Emmaus, Pa. :   Rodale Books, Inc. , 1950.
      (Story Classics.)   167 pp.
        Illustrated with wood engravings by Fritz Eichenberg.
      "About the Author and the Book" by E. J. Fluck.
      Reprinted: A. S. Barnes, 1960.   (Perpetua Books.)
        Contents: "A Terribly Strange Bed" (1852), "The
      Cauldron of Oil" (1861), "The Fatal Cradle" (1861),
      "Mr. Captain and the Nymph" (1876), "Blow Up with
      the Brig" (1859).

"Sister Rose. "   (1855.)

309   Sister Rose.   Philadelphia: Union Press, n. d. (probably pre-1900).

310   Six Letters of Wilkie Collins: From the Charlotte Ashley Felton Memorial Library at Stanford University.
San Francisco: Charles R. Wood and Associates, 1957.
No pagination.
      Introduction by J. Terry Bender, chief of the Division
of Special Collections and keeper of Rare Books, Stanford University Libraries.
      The introduction is a brief biographical sketch and
discussion of the six letters.
      Contents: Six letters, written from 1875 to 1886.
      Contains tipped-in and folded facsimilies of the letters,
and printed transcriptions of the letters.
      The letters discuss mostly business matters.

311   Tales of Suspense.   Ed. Robert Ashley and Herbert van
Thal.   New York: Library Publishers, 1954.   London:
Folio Society, Limited, 1954.   255 pp.
      Lithographs by Anne Scott.

312   Tales of Terror and the Supernatural.   Ed. Herbert van
Thal.   New York: Dover Publications, 1972.   ix + 294
pp.
      Introduction by Herbert van Thal.
      The introduction is a bibliographic biography.   Brief,
but useful, its references to Swinburne (page vi) and
others might confuse a reader unfamiliar with Collins.
      Contents: "The Dream Woman" (1855).   "A Terribly
Strange Bed" (1852).   "The Dead Hand" (1857).   "'Blow
Up with the Brig!'" (1859).   "Mr. Lepel and the House-
keeper" (more commonly known as "The Girl at the
Gate") (1884).   "Miss Bertha and the Yankee" (1877).
"Mr. Policeman and the Cook" (1880).   "Fauntleroy"
(1858).   "A Stolen Letter" (1854).   "The Lady of Glenwith Grange" (1856).   "Mad Monkton" (1855).   "The
Biter Bit" (1858).
      Reviewed by James Mark Purcell (entry 634).

"A Terribly Strange Bed. "   (1852.)

313   A Terribly Strange Bed: Gabriel's Marriage.   London:
Holerth Press, 1924.   (Holerth Library.)   72 pp.

Both stories are from <u>After Dark</u> (1856). "Gabriel's Marriage" was first published in 1853.

314 The Traveller's Story of a Terribly Strange Bed. London: Todd Publishing Company, 1943. (Bantam Books.) 16 pp.

315 _____. London: Vallancey Press, 1944. 16 pp.

"The Yellow Mask." (1855.)

316 The Yellow Mask: A Story. New York: F. M. Lupton Publishing Company, 189-. (Stratford Edition.) 160 pp.

317 The Yellow Mask. Philadelphia: Strawbridge and Clothier, 189-. (Keystone Series of Novels, no. 5.) 176 pp.

318 _____. New York: Daniel Appleton Company, n.d.

319 _____. New York: J. S. Ogilvie Publishing Company, n.d. (1890's?). (Sunset Series.)

320 _____. New York: Federal Book Company, n.d. (1890's?).

321 _____. New York: Hurst and Company, n.d. (1890's?).

322 _____. London: Holerth Press, 1924. (Holerth Library.) 117 pp.

323 _____. London: Staples and Staples, Ltd., 1941.

"The Yellow Tiger." (1857.)

324 The Yellow Tiger: and Other Stories. London: Holerth Press, 1924. (Holerth Library.) 86 pp.

(4.   Short Works and Correspondence, continued)

b.   WORKS IN COLLECTIONS Not Devoted Solely to
     Collins*

                "The Biter Bit. "   (1858.)
     See also entry 456 for another reprint.

325   .   Great Short Stories of Detection, Mystery and
     Horror.   Second Series.   Ed. Dorothy L. Sayers.
     London: Victor Gollancz Ltd. , 1931.   Pp. 216-241
     (total book length: 1147 pp.).
          Introduction by Dorothy L. Sayers.
          Collins is mentioned briefly on page 23 of the intro-
     duction.
          This book also contains "Mad Monkton. "

                "The Captain's Last Love. "   (1876.)

326   The Captain's Last Love: When the Ship Comes In.
     Chicago: Donnelley, Cassette and Loyd, n. d.   (Lake-
     side Library, vol. 4, no. 87.)   Pp. 441-472.
          Illustrated.
          "When the Ship Comes In" is by Walter Besant and
     James Rice.

                "The Dead Alive. "   (1873-1874.)

327   .   Murder by Gaslight: Victorian Tales.   Ed.
     Edward Charles Wagenknecht.   New York: Prentice-
     Hall, 1949.   (Total book length: 437 pp.)
          Introduction by Edward Charles Wagenknecht.
          Reviewed by Kelsey Guilfoil, and in the New York
     Times Book Review (entries 621 and 620).

                "The Dream Woman. "   (1855.)

328   "The Dream Woman. "   The Supernatural Omnibus:

---

*Details on first editions and editions during Collins's lifetime
are in the Bibliographic Essay (the index to which begins on
page 22).   The works in this section are in chronological
order under each heading.

Being a Collection of Stories of Apparitions, Witchcraft, Werewolves, Diabolism, Necromancy, Satanism, Divination, Sorcery, Goetry, Voodoo, Possession, Occult Doom and Destiny. Ed. Montague Summers. London: Victor Gollancz Ltd. , 1931. (Reprinted: 1933, 1949, 1950, 1952, 1956, 1961, 1962.) Pp. 365-387 (total book length: 622 pp.).

The Guilty River.   (1886.)

329 A Guilty River: Fifteen Detective Stories. New York: International Book Company, 189-. (Aldine Edition.) (Total book length: 188 + 145 pp.)
   Illustrated.
   The first 188 pages are occupied by "A Guilty River. "

The Haunted Hotel.   (1878.)

330 The Haunted Hotel: and Twenty-five Other Ghost Stories. New York: Avon, 1941.   (Avon Pocket-Size Books.) (Total book length: 255 pp.)
   Illustrated.

331 "The Haunted Hotel. " Three Supernatural Novels of the Victorian Period. Ed. E. F. Bleiler. New York: Dover Publications, 1975. (Total book length: 325 pp.)

332 No entry.

"Mad Monkton. " (1855.)

333 _____ . Great Stories of Mystery, Detection and Horror. First Series. Ed. Dorothy L. Sayers. London: Victor Gollancz, 1928. (Reprinted, Second Series, 1931.) Pp. 633-690 (total book length: 1147 pp.).
   Introduction by Dorothy Sayers.
   Collins is mentioned briefly on page 23 of the introduction.
   This book also contains "The Biter Bit. "

"Mr. Lismore and the Widow. "   (1883.)

334   .   Stories by English Authors: England.   New
York: Charles Scribner's Sons, 1902.   (Stories by
English Authors.)   Pp. 159-191 (total book length: 207
pp.).

"A Rogue's Life. "   (1856.)

335   A Tale of Two Cities: and A Rogue's Life Written by
Himself.   London: Hutchinson and Company, 1907.
(Hutchinson's Popular Classics.)
A Tale of Two Cities is by Charles Dickens.

"A Terribly Strange Bed. "   (1852.)

336   "The Traveller's Story of a Terribly Strange Bed. "
Stories by English Authors.   New York: Charles Scribner's Sons, 1896.

337   .   Great English Short Stories.   Ed. Lewis Melville and Reginald Hargreaves.   New York: Viking
Press, 1930.   Pp. 591-605 (total book length: xiv +
1047 pp.).
Includes a brief biographical note on pages 591-592.

338   "A Terribly Strange Bed. "   Great Short Stories of the
World: A Collection of Complete Short Stories Chosen
from the Literatures of All Periods and Countries.   Ed.
Barrett H. Clark and Maxim Lieber.   New York: Albert
and Charles Boni, 1931.   (Reprinted: 1932, 1933, 1934,
1935.)   Pp. 178-191 (total book length: xv + 1072 pp.).
"Index": pp. 1069-1072.   "Reading List": p. 1068.
Very short note on Collins, on page 178: "He
[Collins] was rather more interested in the short story
form than Dickens, and a more accomplished master of
it. "

339   .   Spoken Arts SA 1090.   Phonodisc: 12 in. ,
33 1/3 rpm. , 20 min. , 15 sec. , on one side.   (1970?)
Directed by Christopher Casson.

["William Wilkie Collins"]

340   "William Wilkie Collins. "   Warner Library, vol. 7.

Ed. J. W. Cunliffe and A. H. Thorndike.   New York?:
U.S. Publishers Association, 1917.

341   "William Wilkie Collins. " Nineteenth-Century British
Novelists on the Novel.   Ed. George L. Barnett.   New
York: Appleton-Century-Crofts, 1971.   Chapter 15, pp.
142-152 (total book length: xix + 316 pp.).
Introduction by George L. Barnett.
Contents: "Preface" from Antonina: or the Fall of
Rome (1850).   "Dedication" from Basil: A Story of
Modern Life (1852).   "Preface" from The Woman in
White (1861 edition).   "Preface" from Heart and Science
(1883).
Wilkie Collins frequently used his prefaces to defend
himself from what he thought were abusive critics. Bar-
nett's selections are examples of Collins's attempts to
reconcile his art to the criticism of his day.

"Your Money or Your Life. "   (1881.)

342   "Your Money or Your Life: A Tale of My Landlady. "
A Cabinet of Gems: Short Stories from the English
Annuals.   Ed. Bradford Allen Booth.   Berkeley: Uni-
versity of California Press, 1938.   Pp. 333-364 (total
book length: ix + 406 pp.).
Note on Collins on page 334.
Footnoted.

5.   COLLINS'S COLLABORATIONS
WITH CHARLES DICKENS*

The Lazy Tour of Two Idle Apprentices.   (1857.)

See also: Reprinted Pieces ... (entry 349).

343   The Lazy Tour of Two Idle Apprentices: No Thoroughfare: The Perils of Certain English Prisoners.   London:
Chapman and Hall, Ltd. , 1890.   vi + 327 pp.

---

*Details on first editions and editions during Collins's life-
time are in the Bibliographic Essay (the index to which begins on page 22).   The works in this section are in chronological order under each heading.

Illustrated by Arthur Layard.
The Lazy Tour ...: pp. 3-104. No Thoroughfare
(1867): pp. 107-233. The Perils ... (1857): pp. 237-
327.
All three works are collaborations between Collins
and Dickens.

344   Tale of Two Idle Apprentices.   New York: George Munro's Sons, n. d. (1890's?).

345   The Lazy Tour of Two Idle Apprentices.   New York:
P. F. Collier, 1911.   102 pp.

No Thoroughfare.   (1867.)

See also entry 343.

346   . New York: George Munro's Sons, n. d.
(1890's?).

347   No Thoroughfare: Master Humphrey's Clock: and Other
Reprinted Pieces.   Boston: DeWolfe, Fiske, 189-?.
473 pp.
   Illustrated.
   Collins is not given credit for any of the work in
this book.
   Besides No Thoroughfare, the following collaborations
between Collins and Dickens are in this book: The
Wreck of the Golden Mary (1856), The Perils of Certain English Prisoners (1857), The Haunted House
(1859).

The Perils of Certain
English Prisoners.   (1857.)

See also entry 343.

348   The Perils of Certain English Prisoners: A Tale of
Piracy in the West Indies.   London: Thomas Nelson
and Sons, 1923.   191 pp.

349   Reprinted Pieces and The Lazy Tour of Two Idle Ap-
prentices.   New York: Macmillan Company, 1896.
   Introduction by Charles Dickens, Jr.
   Again, Collins is not given credit.

The Wreck of the Golden Mary.   (1856.)

350   The Wreck of the Golden Mary: and Other Stories.
London: J. M. Dent and Sons, Ltd. , 1921.   (King's
Treasuries of Literature Series.)   256 pp.

351   The Wreck of the Golden Mary.   Glasgow: Blackie and
Son, Ltd. , 1935.   (Blackie's English Texts.)   125 pp.

352   _____.   London: Arthur Barker, Ltd. , 1955.   Toronto,
Canada: McClelland and Stewart, Ltd. , 1955.   New
York: Library Publishers, 1956.   158 pp.
      Introduction by Herbert van Thal.
      Illustrated by John Dugan.

353   _____.   Ed. P. Thornhill.   London: Methuen and
Company, Ltd. , 1961.   (Venture Library.)   136 pp.
      Illustrated by John Dugan.

354   The Wreck of the Golden Mary: A Saga of the California Gold Rush.   Kentfield, Calif. :   Allen Press, 1956.
90 pp.
      Illustrated with wood engravings by Blair Hughes-
Stanton.

(Part I, cont.)

PERIODICAL PUBLICATIONS (Works and Correspondence)

355   Blind Love.   The Illustrated London News (July-December 1889).
        Completed by Walter Besant.
        This is the novel's first publication.

356   "Wilkie Collins's Marginalia on His Copy of Forster's Life of Dickens. " Pall Mall Gazette (January 20, 1890).

357   "Wilkie Collins and 'The Frozen Deep. '" The Dickensian, 5 (June 1909), 161.
        This is the publication of a letter from Collins to Mr. Kent (unidentified), dated February 3, 1881. Collins refuses permission for an amateur performance of the play, The Frozen Deep. Anonymous brief remarks accompany the letter.

358   "Some Unpublished Letters of Wilkie Collins: Being Part of the Correspondence of the English Novelist with Paul Hamilton Hayne, the American Poet. " Ed. William H. Hayne. Bookman (American Edition), 37 (March 1913), 66-71.
        Seven letters by Collins are printed. He mostly discusses his poor health.

359   "The Use of Gas in Theatres. " The Mask: A Journal of the Art of the Theatre, 10 (1924), 163-167.
        Reprinted in 1967 by Benjamin Blom, Inc. , of New York. The 1967 reprinting of the periodical, from 1909 through 1929, includes an index compiled by Lorelei F. Guidry.
        "Note on the Essay" and "Biographical Note of Wilkie Collins, " page 163.
        This article by Collins was written in 1881. In 1885 it was printed under the title, The Air and the Audience, by Allen Thordike Rice of New York.
        The article discusses the harmful effect of gaslighting on a theater audience.

360   "A New Collins Letter. "   Saturday Review of Literature,
      3 (August 1927), 30.

          A letter and a short note.

          The note is to Paul Hamilton Hayne, but whether
      Hayne was the recipient of the letter is unclear.   In
      the letter, Collins names Scott, Cooper, and Balzac
      "the three Kings of Fiction. "   He also laments the loss
      of Charles Reade, who died on April 11, 1884.   The
      letter is dated May 3, 1884.

          The letter is included in The University of Texas
      Collection of the Letters of Wilkie Collins, Victorian
      Novelist (entry 362), a dissertation by W. R. Coleman,
      on pages 290-291.   Coleman identifies the recipient of
      the letter as P. H. Hayne.

DISSERTATIONS

361   The Frozen Deep: Under the Management of Mr. Charles
Dickens. Ed. Robert Louis Brannan. Cornell University, 1965. See Dissertation Abstracts, 26 (March
1966), 5429.
     See entries 261 and 260.

362   The University of Texas Collection of the Letters of
Wilkie Collins, Victorian Novelist. Ed. William Rollin
Coleman. University of Texas at Austin, 1975. See
Dissertation Abstracts International, 36 (November 1975),
2789A.
     A useful gathering of 262 letters, spanning the years
1847 to 1889. There are occasional annotations. One
could wish for a more complete index, and for more
thorough annotations.

363   Wilkie Collins as Writer for "Household Words" (1850-
1859), and "All the Year Round" (1859-1870): A Selec-
tion of His Short Stories, Sketches with Headnotes and
Critical Introduction. Ed. Richard David Seiter.
Bowling Green (Ohio) State University, 1970. See Dissertation Abstracts, 31 (October 1970), 1771A.
     Seiter discusses the "neglected lighter side" of Col-
lins's writing. He finds "a subtle but no less delight-
ful humor which can be detected in his later famous
mystery novels" in Collins's shorter works (quotations
from the article in Dissertation Abstracts).

Part II

CRITICISM AND SCHOLARSHIP

BOOKS

1. BOOKS DEVOTED SOLELY TO COLLINS

364   Ashley, Robert Paul. Wilkie Collins. New York: Roy
      Publishers, 1952 (English Novelists Series). London:
      Arthur Barker, Ltd. , 1952 (English Novelists Series).
      Reprinted: Folcroft, Pa. : Folcroft Library Editions,
      1974. New York: Haskell, 1975 (Studies in Fiction,
      no. 34). 144 pp. "Books by Collins": pp. 140-141.
      "Bibliographical Note": pp. 7-9. Indexed.
          A sympathetic attempt to dispel previously published
      inaccuracies, and to reveal something of Wilkie Collins, the
      man. Ashley's book places Collins in critical perspective.
      In some ways Ashley seems self-conscious--he is ever ready
      to do battle with those who underrate Collins's accomplish-
      ments. A useful, well-written book by the leading Collins
      scholar of the post-World War II era. Necessary reading
      for anyone interested in the serious study of Collins; a use-
      ful introduction for students interested in Collins.
          "Wilkie Collins has been the victim of more mis-
      representation and slipshod scholarship than any other English
      novelist of comparable stature ... "--from Ashley's "Preface, "
      page 5.
          "Almost all the portraits penned by the Dickensians
      are vitiated by their jealous dislike of Collins ... " except
      for Hesketh Pearson's Dickens: His Character, Comedy, and
      Career (entry 410)--from "Bibliographical Note, " page 8.
          Reviewed by T. W. Hill, G. F. McCleary, H. C.
      Webster, and in the Spectator and the Times Literary Supple-
      ment (entries 638, 639, 641, 640, 637).

365   Bunnell, William Stanley. Wilkie Collins: The Moon-
      stone. London: James Brodie, 1961. (Notes on Chosen
      English Texts.) 60 pp.

366   Catalogue of the Interesting Library of Modern Books of
      the Late Wilkie Collins, esq. which will be sold at
      auction, by Messrs. Puttick and Simpson ... at their
      gallery ... on Monday, January 29th, 1890.   London:
      1890.   15 pp.   246 items.

367   Davis, Nuel Pharr.   The Life of Wilkie Collins.   Urbana:
      University of Illinois Press, 1956.   360 pp.   "Selected
      Bibliography":   pp. 339-344.   Indexed.
         Illustrated.
         Introduction by Gordon N. Ray, pp. 1-7.
         The biographical materials available on Collins are
few.   His letters to Charles Dickens were destroyed by Dickens.   He seemed to suppress parts of his personal life.
Those who knew him best also seemed to suppress the facts
of Collins's private life.   Davis attempts to penetrate the
mystery of Collins's life by combining possibly autobiographical passages in Collins's work with the known details of Collins's life.
         Davis has been heavily criticized for his failure to
differentiate between conclusions drawn by inference from
Collins's publications and conclusions drawn from more factual sources.   This criticism seems justified.   Davis has
been criticized for his failure to credit Kenneth Robinson
(entry 370) and Robert F. Ashley (entry 364) for their earlier
biographical work.   This criticism is partly justified, but one
should note that Davis's work is clearly an attempt to approach
the character of Collins independent of previous portraits of
the writer.   In this attempt, Davis is only partly successful.
Although he writes with a pleasing style, he is clearly a beginning writer in 1956, and his skills fall short of his ambi-
tious objectives.   This is a book which critics seem to either
love or hate.   It is useful for the serious scholar; it is must
reading for the biographer--because Davis's portrait of Collins is unique; but the inexperienced scholar should use the
book with great caution.   It can be misleading.
         Conjectural.
         Reviewed by Richard D. Altick, Robert P. Ashley,
Bradford Booth, DeLancey Ferguson, Francis Russell Hart,
Edward Wagenknecht, H. Stone, Frederick T. Wood, Lionel
Stevenson, Lauriat Lane, Jr. , and in Time, Notes and
Queries, and the Times Literary Supplement (entries 644-
656).

368   Marshall, William H.   Wilkie Collins.   New York:
      Twayne Publishers, 1970.   (Twayne's English Authors
      Series, 94.)   159 pp.   "Selected Bibliography:"   pp.
      143-153.   Indexed.

This book is an attempt "to deal extensively and ex-
clusively with the literary art of Wilkie Collins and the part
that it played in the development of the English novel"--Mar-
shall's "Preface, " page 5.

This study of Collins's writings is brief, and not as
detailed as one might wish. However, Marshall is superior
to many--perhaps most--of the scholars who have dealt with
Collins, in his meticulous regard for accuracy. His bibliography, for instance, is reliable where most others are not,
and has short and informative annotations.

Marshall asserts that Collins is a minor novelist who
wrote five major works. He identifies the works as The
Woman in White, No Name, Armadale, The Moonstone, and
Man and Wife. He finds in these and Collins's other work,
a broad use of the intellectual currents of the previous three
centuries. The works also show Collins's intellectual and
aesthetic battles with public taste.

The book is carefully written, and can be useful to
anyone interested in studying Collins's works.

369   Page, Norman, ed. Wilkie Collins: The Critical Heri-
      tage. London and Boston: Routledge and Kegan Paul,
      1974. (Critical Heritage Series.) xvi + 288 pp. "Bib-
      liography": pp. 281-282. "Select Index": pp. 283-
      288. "Wilkie Collins: Principal Works": pp. 279-280.
      This book presents an extensive collection of whole
and fragmentary reviews of Collins's books by Collins's contemporary critics. Letters written by Charles Dickens,
George Meredith, and Bishop Thirlwall; articles; and excerpts
from Anthony Trollope's Autobiography are also presented.
      The selections are well chosen. This is a helpful
book.
      Reviewed by Bryan Hulse, Alan Shelston, J. I. M.
Stewart, and in Choice (entries 664, 665, 666, 663).

370   Robinson, Kenneth. Wilkie Collins: A Biography.
      London: John Lane (The Bodley Head), 1951. New
      York: Macmillan Company, 1952. Reprinted: West-
      port, Conn. : Greenwood Press, 1972. London: Davis-
      Poynter Ltd. , 1974. 348 pp. Bibliography: pp. 335-
      339. Indexed.
      Illustrated.
      This is the first and the best of the biographies of
Wilkie Collins. Robinson's portrait of Collins is the most
reliable currently available. The book is the result of pains-
taking research, and in its day revealed information about
the private Collins which had long been unavailable. Robinson

is the first to assemble the many disparate little references
to Collins in the various memoirs, diaries, letters, and
other records which survived through the Victorian era. His
style is straightforward and readable.
    This is the basic biography. It is as close to a
definitive study of Collins's life and career as anything as
yet produced.
    Reviewed by B. Green, Michael Sadleir, Edward
Wagenknecht, T. W. Hill, G. F. McCleary, DeLancey Ferguson, E. L. Walbridge, Robert Phelps, R. P. Ashley,
Naomi Lewis, Carlos Baker, M. M. Bevington, J. P. Kirby,
and in the Times Literary Supplement--in both 1951 and 1974--
and in Newsweek (entries 672-688).

371   Sehlbach, Hans. Untersuchungen über die Romankunst
     von Wilkie Collins. Jena: Verlag der Prommannschen
     Buchhandlung, 1931. (Forschungen zur englischen
     Philologie, 2.) xiv + 184 pp. Bibliography: viii-xiii.
     This book is not very useful.. It is based on a dis-
sertation written at Jena in 1930.

2. INCLUSIONS IN BOOKS
NOT DEVOTED SOLELY TO COLLINS

a. BIOGRAPHICAL

372   Adrian, Arthur A. Georgina Hogarth and the Dickens
     Circle. London: Oxford University Press, 1957. Re-
printed: New York: Kraus Reprint Company, 1971. xvi +
320 pp. "Bibliography": pp. 297-301. "Errata": p. 302.
Indexed.
    Illustrated.
    Contains numerous references to Collins. The por-
tions of the book which deal with Collins's relationship to
The Letters of Charles Dickens (1880-1882) may be of particular interest to scholars.

373   Anderson, Mary [Mme. De Navarro, Mary]. A Few
     Memories. 2 volumes. New York: Harper and
Brothers, 1896. London: Osgood, McIlvaine and Company,
1896. Vol. I: 126 pp. Vol. II: 262 pp. "Index of Names":
259-262. Reprinted: 1 volume, New York: Harper and
Brothers, n.d. (1896?) 262 pp. "Index of Names": pp. 259-
262.

Several tipped-in illustrations.

Anderson discusses Collins on pages 141-147, and on pages 150-151. She repeats, firsthand, Collins's account of his opium addiction's influence on The Moonstone's plot. She mentions Collins's eye affliction. Letters written by Collins to Anderson are reprinted. Anderson holds Collins in high regard.

374 Archer, Frank. An Actor's Notebooks: Being Some Memories, Friendships, Criticisms and Experiences. London: Stanley Paul and Company, 1912. 345 pp. Indexed. Illustrated.

Archer was an actor who performed in Collins's plays, and who was a friend of Collins's for many years. They met in 1873, when Archer played the Reverend Julian Gray in the dramatic version of The New Magdalen.

The book has numerous references to Collins, and reproduces several letters written by Collins to Archer. Archer quotes from a conversation with Collins, and he provides Collins's viewpoints about contemporaries. He gives a sympathetic portrait of Collins; he says of him, "... a good-hearted, loyal, and a very truthful man" (page 304).

Scholars often refer to this work.

375 Bancroft, Marie, and Squire Bancroft. The Bancrofts: Recollections of Sixty Years. London: John Murray, 1909. New York: E. P. Dutton and Company, 1909. xii + 462 pp. Indexed. Illustrated.

Contains a letter by Collins (page 396) and several revealing anecdotes about Collins, all brief.

See entry following (376).

376 Bancroft, Mr. and Mrs. [Squire and Marie Bancroft.] Mr. and Mrs. Bancroft On and Off the Stage. London: R. Bentley and Son, 1889. (Cheaper edition.) (Seventh edition.) 410 pp. No table of contents. First printed: 2 volumes, 1888.

The Bancrofts produced some of Collins's plays. The book contains some biographical information, and two letters written by Collins. The earlier two-volume editions may be easier to use, since they are indexed and have tables of contents.

377 Bancroft, Squire. Empty Chairs. London: John Murray, 1925. ix + 253 pp. Indexed. One plate of Marie Bancroft.

Collins's defense of Edmund Yates when Yates was expelled from the Garrick Club is mentioned (page 103). Collins's addiction to opium is discussed on pages 103-104. He is also mentioned in passing on page 34.

378   Caine, Thomas Henry Hall.   "Wilkie Collins. " My Story.
      London: Heinemann, 1908.   New York: D. Appleton
and Company, 1909.   Chapter VII, pp. 319-335 (total book
length: ix + 402 pp.).   Indexed.
      Illustrated.
      Caine gives insight into Collins's behavior toward
other writers, into his creative processes, and into his conduct in private.   "Indeed, without being the most 'magnetic' of men, Collins was a man to set one at one's ease, to get the best out of one, to send one away with a comfortable feeling toward one's self, and yet a man with a proper sense of personal dignity" (page 324).   Also, "Wilkie had many good stories, and he told them well" (page 326).   Caine also quotes from letters.   A valuable firsthand account.
      Caine is also known simply as Hall Caine.   He was a young writer, and a friend of Collins's in Collins's last years of life.

379   Carrick, T. W.   History of Wigton (Cumberland).   London: Thurnam, Carlisle, 1950?.
      Excerpted in The Dickensian (entry 509).

380   [Cummings, Donald?] "Collins, (William) Wilkie, " by
      D. S. C.   British Authors of the Nineteenth Century.
Ed. Stanley J. Kunitz and Howard Haycraft.   New York: H.
W. Wilson Company, 1936.   Reprinted: 1940, 1948, 1955,
and 1960.   Pp. 144-145.
      A brief biographical essay, with some criticism.

381   Dickens, Charles.   Mr. & Mrs. Charles Dickens: His
      Letters to Her.   Ed. Walter Dexter and Kate Perugini.
London: Constable and Company, 1935.   xvii + 299 pp.   Indexed.
      Foreword by Kate Perugini (the daughter of Mr. and Mrs. Charles Dickens, and first married to Wilkie's brother, Charles).
      Collins is mentioned many times in the letters.

382   Dickens, Charles, Jr.   Reminiscences of My Father.
      New York: Haskell House Publishers, 1973.   32 pp.
      Illustrated.
      Foreword by Mary Angela Dickens (the daughter of

Charles Dickens, Jr.).
    This is a reprint of the rare "Supplement to the
Christmas Windsor" of The Windsor Magazine, 81 (December
1934).   See entry 512.
    This work contains useful biographical material.   The
productions of The Frozen Deep and The Lighthouse are also
mentioned (pages 18-22).
    As one may note, Charles Dickens, Jr. , is the son
of Collins's friend, Charles Dickens.

383   Dickens, Henry Fielding.   The Recollections of Sir Henry
    Dickens, K. C.   London: William Heinemann Ltd. , 1934.
xix + 376 pp.   Indexed.
    Illustrated.
    A portion of the "Preamble" is by Marie Dickens,
the wife of Henry Fielding Dickens.
    Collins is mentioned several times.   H. F. Dickens
is the son of Collins's friend, Charles Dickens.
    The following passage is often cited by scholars: "I
[Henry Fielding Dickens], remember that on one occasion my
father [Charles Dickens], when talking about literature generally, told us there were two scenes in literature which he regarded as being the most dramatic descriptions he could re-
call.   One was fiction, the other history.   The first was the
description of the Woman in White's appearance on the Hamp-
stead Road after her escape from the asylum in Wilkie Collins's famous book The Woman in White.   The other was the
stirring account of the march of the women to Versailles in
Carlyle's French Revolution" (page 54).

384   Dolby, George.   Charles Dickens as I Knew Him: The
    Story of the Reading Tours in Great Britain and America
(1866-1870).   London: Everett and Company, 1912.   (Revised edition.)   xiv + 482 pp.   Indexed.   First published:
1885.   Reprinted: 1887.   xiii + 466 pp.   No index.
    On title page: "By George Dolby: Charles Dickens's
Secretary and Manager. "
    Contains a couple of very brief anecdotes involving
Collins.

385   Downey, Edmund.   Twenty Years Ago.   London: Hurst
    and Blackett, 1905.
    Downey recounts a story told him by his boss, the
publisher William Tinsley (see Tinsley's Random Recollections
of an Old Publisher, entry 418), in which Tinsley describes
his problems with Collins when publishing The Moonstone.
Downey also provides a brief physical description of Collins.

386   Eliot, George.   The George Eliot Letters.   7 volumes.
          Ed. Gordon S. Haight.   New Haven, Conn.:   Yale Uni-
versity Press, 1954-1955.   London: Geoffrey Cumberlege,
Oxford University Press, 1954-1955.
          Collins is mentioned in volumes III, IV, and VI.

387   Elwin, Malcolm.   "Wallflower the Sixth: Wilkie Col-
          lins."   Victorian Wallflowers: A Panoramic Survey of
the Popular Literary Periodicals.   London: Jonathan Cape,
1934.   Reprinted: Port Washington, N.Y.:   Kennikat Press,
1966.   Pp. 203-227 (total book length: 324 pp.).   Indexed.
          Illustrated.
          A speculative, but balanced, account of Collins's
life, with very heavy emphasis on his relationship with Dickens.   Elwin finds the lack of attention paid to Collins prior
to 1934 puzzling.   He identifies The Woman in White, The
Moonstone, No Name, and Armadale as Collins's best work.
          Some remarks of interest, by Elwin: "As a writer,
Collins lack distinction.   At his best, he tells his story
simply and well, occasionally gaining a certain grandeur from
baldness and brevity.   Even at his worst, his plots are remarkable for ingenuity in construction ... " (page 226).   "Collins by rigorously excluding any matter extraneous to the
action and independent of the plot, introduced an economy of
expression upon the lines from which the modern style in
fiction has developed.   Moreover, by virtue of his four principal books, he is the father of the modern 'thriller'.   Ad-
mittedly, he was after Poe, but he was the first to adapt the
weird and extravagant in Poe to the mundane realism of everyday life" (page 227).
          This chapter is a later version of "Wilkie Collins:
The Pioneer of the Thriller, " an article published in the London Mercury in 1931 (entry 513).   Both of the foregoing quotations can be found on page 584 of the magazine version.
Elwin's article is praised by some scholars.

388   Fitzgerald, Percy.   Memories of Charles Dickens: With
          an Account of "Household Words" and "All the Year
Round" and of the Contributors Thereto.   Bristol: J. W.
Arrowsmith Ltd., 1913.   Reprinted: New York: AMS Press
Inc., 1973.   xiv + 383 pp.   Indexed.
          Illustrated.
          On pages 203 and 219 Collins seems something of
an asset to Charles Dickens's endeavors.   On pages 260-264
Fitzgerald creates the picture of Collins as an "elderly" bore,
which is no longer the accepted image of Collins.   Fitzgerald
has an evident distaste for Collins as a man.   His slighting

references, along with John Forster's slighting of Collins
(The Life of Charles Dickens, entry 391), became a dogma
for Dickens scholars. Not until the work of Kenneth Robinson
(Wilkie Collins: A Biography, entry 370) and Robert P. Ashley (see "Wilkie Collins and the Dickensians," entry 588, for
Ashley's most striking attempt to dispel myths which once
surrounded Collins) was Fitzgerald's malicious portrait of
Collins exposed as false.
     If any doubt about the falsehood of Fitzgerald's dis-
cussion of Collins remains, one need only consider the evident and preposterous notion which is the basis of much of
the book: that Fitzgerald, and not Forster or Collins, was
Dickens's closest friend and confidant.
     See also entry following (389).

389   Fitzgerald, Percy. "W. Henry Wills--Wilkie Collins."
       Memoirs of an Author. 2 volumes. London: Richard
Bentley and Son, 1895. Chapter III, pp. 76-96, of vol. 1.
     When discussing Charles Dickens, Fitzgerald remarks
that Collins was among those who "were his [Charles Dickens's] own intimates, who were thoroughly familiar with and
understood his mind ..." (page 6). Later, Fitzgerald states,
"Of all the contributors, the one who had perhaps the largest
share in the success of the journal [Household Words] was
Wilkie Collins, or more correctly William Wilkie Collins.
He was then a rather brilliant young man--pleasant, lively in
talk, of much industry and enthusiasm in his calling" (page
85). "His [Wilkie Collins's] passion for writing was extra-
ordinary" (page 87). Fitzgerald emphasizes the closeness of
Collins's and Dickens's relationship (page 90). He dislikes
The Woman in White (page 91), but acknowledges its popularity.
     This chapter is an odd contrast to Memories of Dick-
ens (entry 388)--although the foundation for the unfriendly--
even cruel--portrait of Collins in the later work can be seen.
Fitzgerald does snipe at Collins, and appears jealous of Collins's achievements. Speculation about the degeneration of
Fitzgerald's descriptions of Collins range from Fitzgerald's
evident jealousy to his probable personal animosity toward
Collins. Perhaps age or the fact that this book was published
by Bentley, Collins's long professional friend, and the later
one was not, had something to do with the shift in Fitzgerald's
portrait.
     Fitzgerald's account of Collins's first public reading
both in this book and in the later book, clearly reflects his
animosity. It is opposed to every other description available
(for instance, that of Frank Archer, entry 374).

390   Fitz-Gerald, S[hafto] J[ustin] Adair. Dickens and the
       Drama: Being an Account of Charles Dickens's Connec-
tion with the Stage and the Stage's Connection with Him.   London: Chapman and Hall, 1910. xxiii + 351 pp. Indexed.
       Illustrated.
       Collins is mentioned briefly many times--mostly des-
criptions of his place in plays produced by Dickens.

391   Forster, John.   The Life of Charles Dickens.   Ed. J.
       W. T. Ley.   London: Cecil Palmer, 1928.   Later ver-
sion: 2 volumes.   Ed. A. J. Hoppé.   London: J. M. Dent
and Sons Ltd. , 1966, and reprinted in 1969.   First printed:
3 volumes, 1972-1874.
       Collins is mentioned several times in this book.   How-
ever, as Ashley, and Marshall (entry 368), and others note,
Collins is seldom mentioned more than in passing.   His relationship with Dickens becomes evident only if one reads
between the lines.
       Kenneth Robinson (entry 370) presents evidence in
his biography of Collins that Forster was jealous of Collins,
and regarded Collins with malice.   Forster had been Dickens's closest friend for years when Collins came into Dickens's life.   When Dickens sought escape from an unhappy
marriage and a demanding professional life, he found Collins
to be a relaxed and congenial companion--Forster, ever the
proper Victorian gentleman, made Dickens feel his disapproval
too frequently.   Forster may well have resented Collins's re-
placing him as Dickens's boon companion.
       Collins evidently thought highly of the biography's
first two volumes.   However, he is quoted as referring to
the work, once the third volume--which essentially ignores
Collins--was published, as "The Life of John Forster with
occasional anecdotes of Charles Dickens" (from Robinson's
Wilkie Collins, page 260; see entry 370).

392   Frith, William Powell.   A Victorian Canvas: Memoirs
       of W. P. Frith, R. A.   Ed. Neville Wallis.   London:
Geoffrey Bles, 1957.   238 pp.   "Bibliography": p. 233.   Indexed.
       Illustrated.
       An abridgement of Frith's My Autobiography.
       Collins is mentioned a few times.   Frith tells an
anecdote which is occasionally cited by scholars on page 220.
A rude guest of Frith's remarks to Collins, "Why, your
novels are read in every back-kitchen in England. " The remark was intended as an insult, but Frith records, "This
Collins heard without a sign of irritation. "

393   Harper, J. Henry.   The House of Harper: A Century
        of Publishing in Franklin Square.   New York: Harper
and Brothers Publishers, 1912.   689 pp.   Indexed.
        Illustrated.
        This book contains useful information about Collins's
publications in the United States and of his visit to America.
        Harper and Brothers was the authorized American
publisher of Collins's work through most of Collins life.

394   Harper, J. Henry.   I Remember.   New York: Harper
        and Brothers, 1934.   Reprinted: Ann Arbor, Mich. :
University Microfilms, 1968.   281 pp.
        Contains a very short anecdote about Collins on pages
168-169.   Collins suffered from "gout of the eyes" (page 169)
and therefore drank only very dry wines.

395   Hawthorne, Julian.   Shapes that Pass: Memories of
        Old Days.   London: Murray, 1928.   Boston and New
York: Houghton Mifflin Company, 1928.   vii + 364 pp.   Indexed.
        A description and anecdote of Collins on pages 169-
170, and on page 227.
        Julian Hawthorne is the son of Nathaniel Hawthorne,
the novelist.

396   Hawtrey, Charles.   The Truth at Last.   Ed. W. Somer-
        set Maugham.   London?:   Thornton Butterworth, 1924.
Boston: Little, Brown, and Company, 1924.   vii + 331 pp.
Indexed.
        Illustrated.
        A firsthand account of the disastrous opening night
of Collins's Rank and Riches (1883), on pages 96-97.

397   Hayter, Alethea.   "Wilkie Collins. "   Opium and the Ro-
        mantic Imagination.   London: Faber and Faber, 1968.
Berkeley and Los Angeles: University of California Press,
1968.   Chapter XI, pp. 255-270 (total book length: 388 pp.).
"References":   p. 343.   Indexed.
        Illustrated.
        Hayter's approach to her subject is straightforward.
She clearly admires much of Collins's work.   She maintains
that opium "alters a writer's power to convey the visual impact of landscape" (page 267), and that Collins is an example
of such altered power.
        She states, "Of all the writers discussed in this book,
Wilkie Collins is perhaps the least like the conventional idea
of a drug addict" (page 269).   She attributes Collins's decline

in his later work to the effects of opium taken over a pro-
longed period of time (pages 269-270): "... though at the
end of his [Collins's] life he was taking quantities [of lauda-
num] large enough to have been fatal to anyone not habituated,
he seems to have been fairly well in control of his habit and
never to have indulged in enormous doses such as Coleridge
and DeQuincey took" (page 256). Hayter adds that Collins
would sometimes take injections of morphine.

    Hayter makes inferences which are not always sup-
ported by her evidence. She attempts to explain, with success, much of Collins's behavior which has been associated
with opium. She refutes some myths.

    Hayter's chapter on Collins is fascinating and illumi-
nating. Her book is controversial, often quoted, and a valuable reference.

398   Hunt, W. Holman. Pre-Raphaelitism and the Pre-
       Raphaelite Brotherhood. 2 volumes. London and New
York: Macmillan, 1905-1906. Vol. I: xxviii + 512 pp.
Vol. II: xiv + 493 pp.
       Illustrated.
       Hunt recounts some anecdotes about, and discusses,
Collins.
       N. P. Davis (The Life of Wilkie Collins, entry 367)
cites Hunt as H. Holman Hunt. The first name is William,
however. Hunt was a member of the Pre-Raphaelite move-
ment.

399   Huxley, Leonard. The House of Smith, Elder. London:
       Printed for Private Circulation, 1923. viii + 249 pp.

400   Hyder, Clyde K. "Wilkie Collins and The Woman in
       White." Victorian Literature: Modern Essays in Criti-
cism. Ed. Austin Wright. New York: Oxford University
Press, 1961. (A Galaxy Book.) Pp. 128-135 (total book
length: iv + 377 pp.). "Selective Index": pp. 372-377.
       Preface by Austin Wright.
       This is a landmark article, a reprint of one first
printed in PMLA, 54 (March 1939), 297-303. See entry 514
for more information.

401   Johnson, Edgar. Charles Dickens: His Tragedy and
       Triumph. 2 volumes. New York: Simon and Schuster,
1952. "Bibliography": vol. 2, pp. xcix-cxv. Indexed.
       Volume 2 is filled with information about Collins.
Johnson's accounts of Collins are thoughtful and enlightening.

402   Johnson, Edgar, and Eleanor Johnson. The Dickens

Theatrical Reader. London: Victor Gollancz Ltd.,
1964. xiv + 370 pp. No index.
    Illustrated.
    Collins is mentioned several times, mostly in re-
printed letters written by Charles Dickens. Chapters "The
Lighthouse" (pages 297-299), "The Frozen Deep" (pages 304-
307), and "No Thoroughfare" (pages 354-356) are of particular
interest.

402a Lambert, Gavin. "Enemy Country Wilkie Collins."
    The Dangerous Edge. London: Barrie and Jenkins,
1975. pp. 1-30. (total book length: xv + 271 pp.) "Bibliography": pp. 271-272. No index.
    Lambert discusses Collins as an outsider in Victorian
society. He also discusses the influence of Collins's childhood on Collins's work.

403 Lehmann, John. Ancestors and Friends. London: Eyre
    and Spottiswoode, 1962. 287 pp. Indexed.
    Illustrated.
    Several anecdotes and much information about Collins
throughout the book. Lehmann quotes from letters written by
Collins. Devotes a chapter to Collins, section III of Part
Four, "A Circle of Friends in the Sixties," pp. 173-180.
    "Of all that circle of friends, it was, I think, Wilkie
Collins who became the most attached, the most closely en-
meshed in my grandparents' [Frederick and Nina Lehmann]
own lives, who poured himself out most spontaneously to
them--to judge at any rate from the letters--and who appeared
the most frequently at the dinner parties and musical evenings,
though his taste in music was different" (page 173).
    Well written.

404 Lehmann, Rudolf. An Artist's Reminiscences. Lon-
    don: Smith, Elder, 1894.

405 Lehmann, R[udolf] C. Charles Dickens as Editor: Being
    Letters Written by Him to William Henry Wills His Sub-
editor. London: Smith, Elder, 1912. xvi + 404 pp. Indexed.
    Illustrated.
    Collins is discussed very often in Dickens's letters.
The close relationship between Collins and Dickens becomes
clear in these letters.

406 Lehmann, R[udolf] C. Memories of Half a Century: A
    Record of Friendships. London: Smith, Elder and

Company, 1908.   x + 362 pp.   Indexed.
      Lehmann quotes from letters written by Collins.   He
provides much material on Collins.   Some discussion of Collins's approach to writing is provided.
      This is an often-cited reference.

407   Lewis, Naomi.   "A Terribly Strange Tale. "   A Visit to
      Mrs. Wilcox.   London: Cresset Press, 1957.   viii +
246 pp.
      A sympathetic and brief biographical essay.   Lewis
draws parallels between Collins's works and his life.   Lewis
finds both "grotesquesness [sic]" (page 126) in Collins's work,
and "novel-writer's poetry" (page 126).
      Some phrases from Lewis's review of Kenneth Robin-
son's Wilkie Collins (entry 370) reappear in this essay (see
entry 680 for the review).
      Lewis opens with: "Two brilliant novels and one
short story (A Terribly Strange Bed) stand out today from the
mass of Wilkie Collins's work and from the heavy silence
that obscures his life" (page 123).
      Reviewed by K. John (entry 662).

      Ley, J. W. T. "Wilkie Collins. "   The Dickens Circle
      (1918).   See entry 482.

408   Marston, Edward.   After Work.
      This work is cited by Kenneth Robinson's Wilkie Col-
lins: A Biography (entry 427) on page 143.   It evidently contains Marston's reminiscences of the first edition publication
of Collins's The Woman in White.   No bibliographic details
are given in Robinson's book and it has proved impossible to
locate a copy of Marston's work.

409   Millais, John Guille.   The Life and Letters of Sir John
      Everett Millais: President of the Royal Academy.   2
volumes.   London: Methuen, 1899.   New York: Frederick
A. Stokes Company, 1899.   Vol. I: xvi + 446 pp.   Vol. II:
xi + 511 pp.   Indexed.
      Illustrated.
      The well-known anecdote of the meeting of Wilkie
Collins, Charles Collins, and John Millais with the Woman
in White is told in volume I, pages 278-279.   A letter from
Collins is printed in volume I, pages 281-282.

410   Pearson, Hesketh.   Dickens: His Character, Comedy,
      and Career.   London: Methuen, 1949.   New York:
Harper and Brothers Publishers, 1949.   361 pp.   "Selected
Sources":   pp. 345-347.

Illustrated.
Collins is portrayed as Dickens's boon companion.
Many brief references to Collins.

411   Pearson, Hesketh. "Mystery Man: (Wilkie Collins,
      1824-89). " Extraordinary People. London: Heinemann
1965.   New York: Harper, 1965.   Chapter 8, pp. 156-164
(total book length: 267 pp.).
      Illustrated.
      This is Hesketh Pearson's last work.   He died short-
ly before its publication.
      The chapter is based substantially on "Victorian Man
of Mystery, " a review of N. P. Davis's The Life of Wilkie
Collins which was published anonymously in the Times Literary Supplement in 1957 (for Davis's book see entry 367 and
for the review see entry 651).   The review material is absent,
and some new remarks are added.
      Reviewed by L. W. Griffin and Christopher Words-
worth (entries 669 and 670).

412   Rawnsley, H. D.   "Charles Dickens in Cumberland. "
      Chapters at the English Lakes.   Glasgow: James Mac-
Lebrose and Sons, 1913.
      Illustrated.
      Discusses Collins's and Dickens's trip in 1857, during
which they gathered material for "The Lazy Tour of Two Idle
Apprentices. " Dickens is Mr. Francis Goodchild and Collins
is Mr. Thomas Idle in the piece.
      Reviewed in The Dickensian (entry 671).

413   Sadleir, Michael.   "The Camel's Back. "   Nineteenth
      Century Essays.   London: Oxford University Press,
1948.

414   [Seccombe, Thomas.]   "Collins, William Wilkie (1824-
      1889), " by T. S.   The Dictionary of National Biblio-
graphy: Founded in 1882 by George Smith.   Ed. Leslie
Stephen and Sidney Lee.   Volume XXII.   Supplement.   London: Oxford University Press, 1917.   Pp. 471-474.   Reprinted: 1921-1922, 1937-1938, 1949-1950, 1959-1960, and
1964-1965.
      The article is a brief presentation of Collins's life
and work.   It is for the most part a good discussion, but is
occasionally unclear.

415   Shore, W. Teignmouth.   "Wilkie Collins. "   Charles
      Dickens and His Friends.   London: Cassell and Company,

1909.   Chapter XXVIII, pp. 195-198.   viii + 323 pp.   No index.

      Illustrated.

      Recounts several anecdotes about Collins.   "A friend tells us that he gained his impulse to write fiction from the perusal of French novels, the art of which appealed strongly to him" (page 196).

      Collins is mentioned elsewhere in the book.

416   Storey, Gladys.   Dickens and Daughter.   London: Muller, 1939.   Reprinted: New York: Haskell House Publishers, 1971.   236 pp.   Indexed.

      Illustrated.

      Storey tells of a time when Dickens's daughter, Kate Perugini, told her of Collins's mistress, Caroline, who was the original for the Woman in White: "She [Kate Perugini] fell into talking about Wilkie Collins who, she recollected, had a mistress called Caroline, a young woman of gentle birth, and the original of the woman in white, in his thrilling novel of that name" (page 213).   "'Poor Wilkie,' Mrs. Perugini continued, 'I liked him, and my father was very fond of him and enjoyed his company more than that of any other of his friends--Forster was very jealous of their relationship'" (page 214).

      Collins is mentioned many times throughout the book.

417   Thompson, Laurence Victor, ed.   Blue Plaque Guide to Historic London Houses and the Lives of Their Famous Residents.   London: Newman Neame, 1953.   pp. 30-31.

      Illustrated.

418   Tinsley, William.   Random Recollections of an Old Publisher.   2 volumes.   London: Simpkin, Marshall, Hamilton, Kent and Company, 1900.

      Tinsley discusses his firm's publication of The Moonstone, and the public reaction to the novel.

419   Walford, L. B.   Memories of Victorian London.   London: Edward Arnold, 1912.   xii + 351 pp.   Indexed.

      Collins is discussed on pages 60 through 63 and pages 206 through 214.   The former passage contains anecdotes about Collins's life as a schoolboy, related to Walford (then Lucy Colquhoun).   She recounts anecdotes told by Collins about the press in the United States.   Includes some discussion of his friendships.

420   Ward, Mrs. E. M.   Memories of Ninety Years.   Ed.

Isabel G. McAllister.   London: Hutchinson and Company,
n. d. (1933?).   24 + 332 pp.   Indexed.
Illustrated.
On pages 38 through 40 Mrs. (Henrietta) Ward re-
counts the story of her elopement with Edward Matthew Ward
and Collins's involvement in it.   Wilkie arranged many of the
details.
A letter by Collins about Edward's illness is reprinted
on page 195.   The book also includes anecdotes about Collins
and his family.

421   Winter, William. "Wilkie Collins. "   Old Friends:
Being Literary Recollections of Other Days.   New York:
Moffat, Yard, and Company, 1909.   Chapter VIII, pp. 203-
222 (total book length: 407 pp.).   Indexed.
Illustrated.
"To be in his [Collins's] society was to be charmed,
delighted, stimulated, and refreshed" (page 203).
A very favorable description of Collins by a friend
who admired him greatly.   Letters by Collins written to Winter are reprinted.   Winter discusses Collins's use of laudanum
(page 211).   Collins tells Winter that he was blind with pain
when writing The Moonstone, and dictated the novel to a number of clerks.
Collins is also discussed in other chapters.
Oddly enough, this account was pretty much ignored
by scholars until Kenneth Robinson used it in his biography
of Collins (entry 370).   It is a valuable firsthand account of
Collins--and Winter praises Collins's characters (page 215),
a point of view which went against the critical dogma of the
early Twentieth Century.

422   Wright, Thomas. Life of Charles Dickens.   New York:
Charles Scribner's Sons, 1936.   392 pp.   Bibliography:
pp. 377-385.

(2.   Inclusions in Books ... , continued)

b.   BIBLIOGRAPHICAL

423   Ashley, Robert P.   "Wilkie Collins. "   Victorian Fiction:
A Guide to Research.   Ed. Lionel Stevenson.   Cambridge, Mass.: Harvard University Press, 1964.   Pp. 277-
284, part of Chapter 8.   "Bibliography and Editions": pp.

277-280 (total book length: vi + 440 pp.).   Indexed.
        Ashley's article is the first half of a chapter on Col-
lins and Charles Reade (see Wayne Burns, "Charles Reade, "
entry 403).   Ashley indicates that the Collins materials are
essentially covered by scholarship.
        Ashley has redone the Collins entry for a new, as
of this writing unpublished, edition of Victorian Fiction.

424   Brussel, I. R.   "Wilkie Collins. "   Anglo-American
        First Editions, 1826-1900.   Volume I (of 2 vols.).   Lon-
don: Constable and Company, 1935.   New York: R. R. Bow-
ker Company, 1935.   (Bibliographia Series, No. 9.)
        Introduction to Volume I by Graham Pollard.
        Pollard asserts that I. R. Brussel "has, in fact,
made the first step toward a bibliography of American literary
piracy" (page 3).   Pollard mentions Collins occasionally, and
quotes from letters written by Collins (pages 13 and 14-15).
        Volume I is a bibliography of books written by Eng-
lish authors, and first published in the United States.   Brussel provides an analytical bibliography of twenty-four of Collins's works, including The Woman in White, Armadale, The
Dream Woman, The Dead Alive, A Rogue's Life, Jezebel's
Daughter, Love's Random Shot, The Evil Genius, and The
Legacy of Cain.   The notations are detailed and informative.
        Reviewed in the Times Literary Supplement, entry
642.

425   Cordasco, Francesco, and Kenneth W. Scott.   Wilkie
        Collins and Charles Reade: A Bibliography of Critical
Notices and Studies.   Brooklyn, N. Y. :   Long Island University Press, 1949.   vi + 7 pp.
        Grossly inaccurate.   Terribly incomplete.   Includes
works in its list which have no mention of either Wilkie Collins or Charles Reade.   The entries which concern Collins
are mixed with those which concern Reade, and are rarely
differentiated one from the other.

426   Elton, Oliver.   "Charles Dickens, Wilkie Collins,
        Charles Reade. "   A Survey of English Literature:
1830-1880.   Volume II.   London: Edward Arnold, Ltd. ,
1920.   Reprinted: 1926, 1932, 1948, 1955, 1961, and 1965.
Pp. 194-230 (total book length: xi + 432 pp.).   Indexed.
        Collins on pages 221-223.
        Of little consequence.

427   Hardy, Barbara.   Revised by Malcolm Y. Andrews.
        "Collins, William Wilkie. "   Cassell's Encyclopedia of

World Literature. Ed. S. H. Steinberg. Volume II. Revised and enlarged, general editor, J. Buchanan-Brown. New
York: William Morrow and Company, 1973. P. 319.
    Very brief bibliographic note on Collins.

428   Magill, Frank Northen, ed. Cyclopedia of World Authors.
    New York: Harper, 1958. Reprinted: Englewood Cliffs,
N. J.: Salem Press, 1974 (revised edition). Pp. 227-229.

429   Nisbet, Ada. "Charles Dickens." Victorian Fiction:
    A Guide to Research. Ed. Lionel Stevenson. Cam-
bridge, Mass.: Harvard University Press, 1964. Pp. 44-
153 (total book length: vi + 440 pp.). Indexed.
    Contains listing of comparative studies of Dickens
and Collins, pages 110-111. Has other references to Collins.

430   Parrish, M. L., with the assistance of Elizabeth V.
    Miller. Wilkie Collins and Charles Reade: First Edi-
tions Described with Notes. London: Constable and Company,
1940. Reprinted: Burt Franklin, 1968 (Bibliography and
Reference Series 186). x + 355 pp.
    Illustrated. Contains facsimiles of letters and posters
for Collins's plays.
    A landmark work. An analytical bibliography of first
editions. Includes five posthumous publications of Collins's
work, the latest in 1923.
    Although not quite complete, this is a very valuable
and significant work. It is pivotal in the progress of research into Collins's works. It is filled with useful information. Copious notes are provided. A few inaccuracies.
    Reviewed by D. Randall and in the Times Literary
Supplement (see entries 668 and 667).

431/2 Quayle, Eric. "Charles Dickens and Wilkie Collins."
    The Collector's Book of Detective Fiction. London:
Studio Vista, 1972. Pp. 42-50 (total book length: 143 pp.).
"Bibliography": p. 129. Indexed.
    Photographs by Gabriel Munro.
    Heavily illustrated.
    This book is a bibliophile's delight. It is a biblio-
graphic history, with criticism. The plot and characterization in The Moonstone are praised.
    "Much of the credit for creating the modern detective
novel belongs, in almost equal fashion, to Charles Dickens
and Wilkie Collins" (page 50).
    Collins is mentioned elsewhere in the book.
    Much fun.

Quilter, Harry.   "Wilkie Collins. " Preferences in Art,
Life, and Literature (1892).   See entry 453.

433   Sadleir, Michael.   XIX Century Fiction: A Bibliographi-
      cal Record Based on His Own Collection.   2 volumes.
London: Constable and Company, 1951.   Los Angeles: University of California Press, 1951.   Vol. I: xxxiii + 399 pp.
Indexed.   Vol. II: 195 pp.   Indexed.
      Illustrated.
      Volume I: "Comparative Scarcities: Collins, Wilkie, "
pp. 376-377.   A brief discussion of bibliographic problems
when dealing with certain of Collins's works.
      Also in Volume I: "An Author-Alphabet of First
Editions: Collins, W. Wilkie (1824-1889), " pp. 93-95.   Brief
analytical bibliographical descriptions of many (but not all) of
Collins's books in first editions.
      Volume II: "Yellow-Back Collection: Collins, Wilkie, "
p. 27.   Lists several of Collins's books published "in yellow-
back pictorial boards" (page 27), and large format, and one
book published with an orange back.

434   Sadleir, Michael.   "Wilkie Collins, 1824-1889. "   Excur-
      sions in Victorian Bibliography.   London: Chaundy and
Cox, 1922.   Reprinted: Folcroft, Pa. : Folcroft Press,
1969.   London: Dawsons, 1974.   Pp. 129-155 (total book
length: vii + 240 pp.).   "Index of Book-Titles": pp. 235-240.
      Critical essay, "Wilkie Collins, " on pages 129-135.
In it, Sadleir describes Collins as a fine story teller, but a
second-rate artist.   Each of Collins's characters is a mere
"marionette" (page 131); Collins "is inferior as a painter of
life to many writers of his time whose very existence is now-
adays forgotten. "
      "Editiones Principes" on pages 136-155, an analytical
bibliography of first editions of novels and plays.
      Well liked by some scholars.

435   Sayers, Dorothy.   "William Wilkie Collins (1824-1889). "
      The Cambridge Bibliography of English Literature.
Volume III, 1800-1900.   London: Cambridge University Press,
1940.   pp. 480-482.
      Bibliography of works and items about Collins.   Very
incomplete.
      See also the anonymous entries in the Supplement and
The New Cambridge Bibliography of Literature (entries 438
and 437).

436   Schulz, H. C.   English Literary Manuscripts in the

Huntington Library.   San Marino, Calif. :   Henry E.
Huntington Library, 1968.   Reprinted from The Huntington
Quarterly.   See entry 528 for list of Collins's manu-
scripts.

437   "William Wilkie Collins. "   The New Cambridge Biblio-
      graphy of English Literature.   Volume 3.   1800-1900.
Ed. George Watson.   London: Cambridge University Press,
1969.   pp. 924-928.
        See entry 438 and Dorothy L. Sayers's article in the
1940 edition of this work, entry 435.

438   "William Wilkie Collins (1824-1889). "   The Cambridge
      Bibliography of English Literature.   Volume V.   Supple-
ment: A. D. 600-1900.   Ed. George Watson.   London: Cambridge University Press, 1957.   p. 637.
        See entry 437 and Dorothy L. Sayers's article in the
1940 edition of this work, entry 435.

(2.   Inclusions in Books ... , continued)

c.   ASSESSMENTS OF COLLINS'S LIFE AND WORKS

439   Buchloh, Paul G.   "Der viktorianische Detektivroman:
      Dickens und Collins. "   Der Detektivroman: Studien zur
Geschichte und Form der englischen und amerikanischen
Detektivliteratur.   Paul G. Buchloh and Jens P. Becker.
Darmstadt: Wissenschaftliche Buchgesellschaft, 1973.   Chapter
III, pp. 47-56 (total book length: 199 pp.).   Bibliography:
pp. 159-184.
        A look at Dickens's and Collins's work as typical of
Victorian mysteries.   The Woman in White is seen as the
progenitor of the big push in the popularity of detective fiction.

440   Chesterton, G. K.   The Victorian Age in Literature.
      New York: H. Holt and Company, 1913.   London:
Williams and Norgate, 1913.   (Home University Library of
Modern Knowledge, no. 61.)   vi + 256 pp.   "Bibliographical
note": pp. 253-254.
        Collins is mentioned briefly on pages 130 through
132.
        "Wilkie Collins may be said to be in this way a
lesser Dickens ... " (page 130).
        "Wilkie Collins is chiefly typical of his time in this

respect: that while his moral and religious conceptions were as mechanical as his carefully constructed fictitious conspiracies, he nevertheless informed the latter with a sort of involuntary mysticism which dealt wholly with the darker side of the soul" (page 130).

"His [Collins's] ghosts do walk. They are alive; and walk as softly as Count Fosco, but as solidly" (page 132).

"Finally, The Moonstone is probably the best detective tale in the world" (page 132).

441   Cooke, John Daniel, and Lionel Stevenson. "Wilkie Collins (1824-1889)." English Literature of the Victorian Period. New York: Appleton-Century-Crofts, 1949. New York: Russell and Russell, 1971. (Appleton-Century Handbooks of Literature.) Pp. 284-286 (total book length: xii + 438 pp.). Bibliography: pp. 423-425. Indexed.

Illustrated.

A short biographical sketch.

"Collins was the first novelist who gave primary importance to ingenious plot structure" (page 285).

"His novels had an immediate effect upon those of Dickens, who borrowed some of Collins's devices for his later works. On the other hand, Collins was a follower of Dickens in his methods of characterization ... " (page 285).

442   de la Mare, Walter. "The Early Novels of Wilkie Collins." The Eighteen-Sixties: Essays by Fellows of the Royal Society of Literature. Ed. John Drinkwater. New York: Macmillan, 1932. London: The Cambridge University Press, 1932. Tokyo: Maruzen Company, 1932. Pp. 51-101 (total book length: x + 282 pp.). Indexed.

A personable essay. It reveals much of the subtlety and depth of Collins's early novels. De la Mare points out Collins's ability to write brilliant prose. He also portrays Collins as a fine craftsman plagued by inconsistency. While de la Mare notes Collins's strengths and weaknesses, and his essay is genuinely revealing of the quality of the works discussed, he gives few answers to questions which arise. For instance, he describes the general weakness of Collins's young male characters, and describes the unusual strength of his young women, but offers little by way of explanation for these qualities.

This essay is highly praised by many scholars--although Lionel Trilling damns it.

Reviewed by Lionel Trilling, Yvonne ffrench, Forrest Reid, and in Notes and Queries and the Times Literary Supplement (entries 661, 658, 660, 659, 657).

91   Inclusions in Books

443   Eliot, T. S.   "Wilkie Collins and Dickens. "   Selected
Essays: 1917-1932.   London: Faber and Faber, 1932.
New York: Harcourt, Brace, and Company, 1932. Reprinted:
1936 and 1947. Pp. 373-382 (total book length x + 415 pp.).
The article is reprinted in: Selected Essays: New Edition.
New York: Harcourt, Brace and World, Inc. , 1950. Reprinted: 1960 and 1964. Pp. 409-418 (total book length:
xiv + 460 pp.). The article is also reprinted in: The Victorian Novel: Modern Essays in Criticism. Ed. Ian Watt.
London: Oxford University Press, 1971. Pp. 133-141 (total
book length: ix + 485 pp.). No index.
    Based on the article, "Wilkie Collins and Dickens, "
published in the Times Literary Supplement in 1927 (see entry
541). This article is also the basis for the introduction to
Collins's The Moonstone, published by the Oxford University
Press in 1928 (see entry 145).
    An interesting comparative study. Eliot finds Collins's
strongest influence in Dickens's Bleak House. He finds Dickens's strongest influence in Collins's The Woman in White.
Eliot provides a general study of Collins's prose's strengths
and weaknesses. He refers to Dickens's and Collins's novels
as "melodramas. "
    "The Moonstone is the first and greatest of English
detective novels" (page 413, New Edition).
    "The Moonstone is very near to Bleak House. The
theft of a diamond has some of the same blighting effect on
the lives about it as the suit in Chancery; Rosanna Spearman
is destroyed by the diamond as Miss Flite is destroyed by
Chancery" (page 418, New Edition).

444   Ellis, S. M.   "Wilkie Collins. "   Wilkie Collins, Le
    Fanu and Others.   London: Constable and Company,
1931. Reprinted: 1935, 1937, and 1951. New York: Ray
Long and Richard R. Smith, 1931. Reprinted: Bombay, Cal-
cutta, and Madras: Orient Longmans, Ltd. , 1951. Toronto:
Longmans, Green and Company, 1951. Cape Town and Nairo-
bi: Longmans, Green and Company, 1951. Pp. 1-53 (total
book length: 343 pp.).
    Illustrated.
    Praises Collins and discusses Collins's influence on
Charles Dickens, A Chapter on Wilkie's brother, "Charles
Allston Collins, " is included on pages 54-73.
    This has long been a standard reference work for
scholars.

    Elwin, Malcolm. "Wallflower the Sixth: Wilkie Col-
    lins. " Victorian Wallflowers (1934). See entry 387.

445   Gerould, Gordon Hall. "Variations in Romance." <u>The Patterns of English and American Fiction: A History.</u> Boston: Little, Brown and Company, 1942. Pp. 394-419 (total book length: x + 526 pp.). "Bibliography": pp. 493-504. Indexed.

        Illustrated.

        Praises <u>The Woman in White</u>, <u>Armadale</u>, and <u>The Moonstone.</u> Collins is contrasted with Arthur Conan Doyle on pages 417 and 418. Collins's influence on Thomas Hardy is mentioned briefly on pages 385-386.

        "... Wilkie Collins (1824-89) may properly be said to have given the writing of romance a new direction and to have an influence of which the end is not yet in sight" (page 397).

        Well researched and pleasant reading.

446   Hardy, Thomas J. "The Romance of Crime." <u>Books on the Shelf.</u> London: Philip Allan, 1934. Chapter XII, pp. 219-235 (total book length: 253 pp.). Indexed.

        Hardy credits <u>The Woman in White</u> with being the first novel "that made the new scientific outlook and method its own" (page 223). He discusses Collins's art of novel construction. He disagrees with those who derogate the literary merit of Collins's work. (Hardy disagrees principally with George Saintsbury's remarks in <u>The English Novel</u>--entry 454--and <u>Nineteenth Century Literature</u>--entry 503.) Hardy writes that Collins's "reputation has unjustly suffered... " (page 225). Also, "Collins was too true an artist, too acute an explorer in the then unworked vein of psychology to be dismissed with a few references to melodrama and clumsy contrivance" (page 226).

        This is an unusually independent essay. Hardy also asserts that Collins influenced Charles Dickens, Gaboriau and du Boisgobey of France, and through the French, Anna Katharine Green of the United States. The styles of Collins and Arthur Conan Doyle are also compared. Hardy principally discusses Collins's works written between 1860 and 1868.

        Although the content of this work has intrinsic value, it also serves as one more indication that the scholarly community's expanded interest in Collins in the late 1940's was not a sudden revival of interest, but was the result of many years of gradual progress finally coming to fruition.

447   Haycraft, Howard. <u>Murder for Pleasure: The Life and Times of the Detective Story.</u> New York and London: D. Appleton-Century Company, 1941. xviii + 409 pp. Indexed.

Illustrated.
"In the opinion of many able critics, in fact, Collins
was almost Dickens' equal in characterization and was often
his superior in technical plot construction" (page 37).   These
critics are not identified by Haycraft.
"... [Collins] fell into obscurity in his last years and
died ungratefully forgotten in his own lifetime" (page 37).
This assertion has been utterly refuted.   See Kenneth Robin-
son's Wilkie Collins: A Biography (entry 370), Robert Ashley's
Wilkie Collins (entry 364), Nuel Pharr Davis's The Life of
Wilkie Collins (entry 367), or the "Bibliographic Essay" at
the beginning of the present work.
Haycraft asserts that The Moonstone is "directly
paraphrased in several modern works, including, among
others, two of the finest detective novels of this generation:
Dorothy Sayers' The Documents in the Case and Michael
Innes' Lament for a Maker" (page 39).
Some of Haycraft's assertions have been supplanted
and disproved by subsequent scholarship.   His remarks are
interesting, but can grossly mislead the uninformed reader.

448   Knoepflmacher, U. C.   "The Counterworld of Victorian
Fiction and The Woman in White. "   The Worlds of Victorian Fiction.   Ed. Jerome H. Buckley.   Cambridge, Mass. ,
and London: Harvard University Press, 1975.   (Harvard
English Studies 6.) Pp. 351-369 (total book length: x + 416
pp.).
This book is part of an annual series of books some
libraries list as a serial (or periodical).   In these libraries
it would be cited as Harvard University Studies, 6 (1975).
Knoepflmacher begins his essay with a quotation
from The Rebel by Camus, which asserts that the novel is
the product of a historically recent romantic and rebellious
imagination; but, Knoepflmacher points out, Camus ignores
the Victorian novel when he examines specimens of the
novel.   The evidence of the Victorian novelists' distrust of
defiance and escapism is, Knoepflmacher believes, super-
ficial.   Beneath the Victorian novel's orderly surface "lurks
a vital 'counterworld' that is asocial and amoral, unbound by
the restraints of the socialized superego" (page 352).   Even
though the novelists tried to suppress the anarchic qualities
of their works, the power in many great Victorian novels
lies in "traces of an anarchic 'intelligence' ... " (page 352).
Knoepflmacher finds The Woman in White to be "a unique
instance" (page 353) in which the anarchic world is openly
portrayed as "a powerfully attractive alternative" (page 353)
to the conventional order of the "civilized world" (page 353).

Knoepflmacher finds a depiction of "lawful order"
colliding with "anarchic lawlessness" (page 362) in The Woman
in White. His analysis of the processes involved in civilized
characters' becoming uncivilized is interesting. His discussion of "a universe at variance with middle-class Victorian"
mores, as asserted by the character Fosco, is revealing.
Collins's skill and art are treated.

The counterworld of the Victorian novel is not a new
idea--nonetheless, this is one of the best essays written about
Collins's work. It can be very helpful to the beginning scholar
and others who are unfamiliar with Collins. This is an in-
sightful treatment of Collins.

Lewis, Naomi. "A Terribly Strange Tale. " A Visit to
Mrs. Wilcox (1957). See entry 407.

449   Lovett, Robert Morss, and Helen Sard Hughes. "Dickens and His School. " The History of the Novel in England. Boston: Houghton Mifflin Company, 1932. Chapter
X, 221-255 (total book length: 495 pp.). Bibliography: pp.
465-479. Indexed.

A section, "William Wilkie Collins (1824-89), " is
devoted to Collins on pages 250-255.

"His [Collins's] success is attested by the number
of his imitators, in his own day and in ours" (page 250).

This article emphasizes Collins's concern with the
plots of his novels. It is a mundane item, which repeats
what had already been written about Collins. It is even-
handed, but unoriginal: Collins wrote good plots, but poor
characterizations.

450   Melville, Lewis. "Wilkie Collins. " Victorian Novelists.
London: Archibald Constable and Company, 1906. Reprinted: Folcroft, Pa. : Folcroft Press, 1970. Pp. 125-
145 (total book length: 321 pp.).
Illustrated.

"He [Collins] was a man old before his time, with
his health wasted and his powers of creation dimmed; and
though he wrote more than a dozen novels after The New
Magdalen, it is said that in his later years the pens of kind-
ly companions helped his failing vigour to keep pace with the
demands of the market" (page 126). The suggestion that
ghost writers helped Collins is vigorously denied by Kenneth
Robinson in Wilkie Collins: A Biography (pages 303-304; see
entry 370), and textual evidence contradicts the suggestion.
Robinson identifies Waugh as the first to put in print the idea
that Collins used ghost writers (see entry 548 for Waugh's

article, "Wilkie Collins and His Mantle").
    Melville asserts, "Yet, though living when famous
novelists flourished, he [Collins] was the greatest story-teller
of them all" (pages 126-127).   Also, "He [Collins] has no
claim to rank with the greatest, but at his best he told a
story with a simple directness of purpose that has never perhaps been equalled, and has certainly never been excelled by
any English writer of fiction" (page 145).

    Murch, A. E.   "Detective Themes in the Works of
    Charles Dickens and Wilkie Collins. "   The Development
of the Detective Novel (1958).   See entry 474.

451   Ousby, Ian.   "Wilkie Collins and Other Sensation Novelists. "   Bloodhounds of Heaven: The Detective in English
Fiction from Godwin to Doyle.   Cambridge, Mass. , and London: Harvard University Press, 1976.   Pp. 111-136 (total
book length: x + 194 pp.).   Indexed.
    Illustrated.
    Ousby discusses The Moonstone and Sergeant Cuff at
length.   He discusses other works and characters, and places
Collins in a relationship to Dickens and other writers.   Ousby
finds points of interest in Collins's later works--especially
"My Lady's Money" (1877), The Law and the Lady (1875),
and "I Say No" (1884).
    Collins is mentioned briefly in other chapters of this
book.

452   Pritchett, V. S.   "The Roots of Detection. "   Books in
    General.   London: Chatto and Windus, 1953.   Chapter
24, pp. 179-184 (total book length: viii + 258 pp.).   "Bibliography": pp. 255-258.
    Pritchett discusses Collins and the development of
detective fiction.   He also gives a brief and intelligent discussion of The Moonstone.   He praises both The Moonstone
and Collins's characterizations.
    "Wilkie Collins is, at any rate, the first properly
uniformed and impressive detective novelist in English literature" (page 179).
    "The Moonstone is the first and last of the detective
novels, and I would like to ask the addicts what more has
really been added to the genre since his [Collins's] time"
(page 184).

    Quayle, Eric.   "Charles Dickens and Wilkie Collins. "
    The Collector's Book of Detective Fiction (1972).   See
entry 431.

453   Quilter, Harry.   "Wilkie Collins. "   Preferences in Art,
   Life, and Literature.   London: Swan Sonnenschein and
Company, 1892.   Chapter XI, pp. 247-280 (total book length:
xvi + 404 pp.). "Index of Proper Names":   pp. 401-404.
      Heavily and beautifully illustrated.
      The title of this work has been cited incorrectly in
a couple of the standard bibliographies of Victorian studies.
      Titled on page 247: "In Memoriam Amici: Wilkie
Collins. "
      Quilter was a young writer and critic when he wrote
"A Living Story-Teller, " which was published in Contemporary
Review in 1887 (see "Bibliographic Essay" for more information).   The article was about Collins, and praised the by then
critically neglected author.   Just as he had often done with
other young writers, Collins helped Quilter with his writing,
and the two became friends.
      This article, "Wilkie Collins, " is based partly on
"A Living Story-Teller. "   It is a critical essay filled with
praise for Collins.   Quilter examines Collins's novels in detail.   He relates Collins's "pictures" (backgrounds) to "landscape" painting, and claims a common relationship between
the effect upon an audience's emotion of Collins's "pictures"
and "landscape" painting.
      Quilter includes a short annotated bibliography of
Collins's works.   He concludes with some praise for Collins's character--as one who was generous and helpful to
others.   He feels critics were unfair to Collins, and he remarks on Collins's popularity in countries other than England.

      Sadleir, Michael.   "Wilkie Collins, 1824-1889. "   Ex-
      cursions in Victorian Bibliography (1922). See entry 434.

454   Saintsbury, George.   The English Novel.   London: Dent
   and Sons, 1913.
      Contains derogatory remarks about Collins.   Quoted
and refuted by Thomas J. Hardy in "The Romance of Crime, "
in Books on the Shelf (entry 446).

455   Sayers, Dorothy L.   "Introduction. "   The Omnibus of
   Crime.   Ed. Dorothy L. Sayers.   New York: Payson
and Clarke Ltd. , 1929.   Pp. 9-47 (total book length: 1177
pp.).
      "Taking everything into consideration, The Moonstone
is probably the very finest detective story ever written" (page
25).
      Sayers praises Collins's careful plotting.   The dis-
cussion of Collins is brief and very favorable.

This introduction has often been praised--notably by
Robert P. Ashley (entries 364 and 423) and William H. Marshall (entry 368).

456   Sayers, Dorothy L.   "Introduction. "   Tales of Detection.
      London: J. M. Dent and Sons, Ltd. , 1936.   New York:
E. P. Dutton and Company, 1936.   (Everyman's Library.)
Pp. vii-xiv (total book length: xvi + 382 pp.).
      Sayers briefly discusses Collins on pages ix-x, with
an emphasis on The Moonstone.   She praises his plotting and
characterization.
      This introduction is frequently alluded to by scholars.
      The book contains Collins's "The Biter Bit" on pages
20-48.

      [Seccombe, Thomas.]   "Collins, William Wilkie (1824-
      1889), " by T. S.   The Dictionary of National Biblio-
graphy (vol. XXII, Supplement; 1917).   See entry 414.

457   "STET" [Thomas Earle Welby].   Back Numbers.   Lon-
      don: Constable and Company, 1929.   Pp. 177-181 (total
book length: xi + 226 pp.).   No index.
      STET finds Collins to be a "satisfactory" novelist,
but not a "great" novelist (page 179).
      "The real Wilkie Collins was a dealer in plots, not
a critic of life" (page 178).

458   Swinburne, Algernon Charles.   "Wilkie Collins. "
      Studies in Prose and Poetry.   London: Chatto and Win-
dus, 1894.   Pp. 110-128 (total book length: 298 pp.).   Reprinted in: The Complete Works of Algernon Charles Swinburne.   Volume 15.   Ed. Edmund Gosse and Thomas James
Wise.   London: William Heinemann Ltd. , 1926.   New York:
Gabriel Wells, 1926.   (Bonchurch Edition.)   Pp. 289-306
(total book length: 466 pp.).
      Reprinted from "Wilkie Collins. "   The Fortnightly
Review.   See entry 546 for annotation.

459   Symons, Julian.   "Dickens, Collins, Gaboriau: the
      Pattern Forms. "   Bloody Murder: From the Detective
Story to the Crime Novel: A History.   London: Faber and
Faber, 1972.   Chapter 3, pp. 42-57 (total book length: 254
pp.).   "Index of Books and Short Stories": pp. 244-249.
"Index of Authors and Names": pp. 250-254.
      "Collins is generally regarded, as he was in his own
lifetime, as a writer whose merits lie purely in the field of
melodrama" (page 48).

Symons praises "Anne Rodway" (1856) and "The Biter Bit" (1858) from The Queen of Hearts (1859) on page 49.   He points out that "A Stolen Letter" (1854) "follows Poe's device in 'The Purloined Letter' so closely that it can almost be called a crib" (page 49).   He praises The Woman in White (pages 49-50) and The Moonstone (pages 51-52).

He discusses The Notting Hill Mystery by Charles Felix as a detective novel (1862-1863) which predates The Moonstone.   He calls The Law and the Lady (1875) "sur-prisingly neglected" (page 54).

This is a sophisticated, well-researched, if short, discussion of Collins's work.   It can be a useful reference.

Collins is mentioned elsewhere in the book.

460   Tillotson, Kathleen.   "The Lighter Reading of the Eighteen-Sixties. "   The Woman in White by Wilkie Col-lins.   Ed. Anthea Trodd.   Boston: Houghton Mifflin Company, 1969.   Pp. ix-xxvi.

The introduction to this edition of The Woman in White.

A concise discussion of the early development of the sensation novel.   It helps to place The Woman in White and Collins into perspective in the literary trends of the 1860's.

461   Wagenknecht, Edward Charles.   "The Disciples of Dickens. "   Cavalcade of the English Novel: From Elizabeth to George VI.   New York: Holt, Rinehart and Win-ston, 1943.   Reprinted: 1954.   Pp. 234-267 (total book length: xviii + 686 pp.).   "Index of Names":   pp. 661-671. "Index of Titles":   pp. 672-686.

"Wilkie Collins, " pages 236-243.

An appreciation of Collins's works.

462   Walker, Hugh.   The Literature of the Victorian Era. Cambridge, England: Cambridge University Press, 1910.   viii + 1067 pp.   Indexed.

Collins is very briefly discussed and evaluated.

463   Weygandt, Cornelius.   "The Followers of Scott and the Earlier Victorians. "   A Century of the English Novel. New York: Century Company, 1925.   Chapter IX, pp. 122-171 (total book length: 504 pp.).   Indexed.

'Wilkie Collins, " pages 168-171.

Weygandt compares Collins unfavorably with Trollope (page 169) and Doyle (page 170).   This is a brief, bitter, and unsubstantiated attack on Collins.

"In plot and plot alone, of all the qualifications of

the novelist, has he [Collins] succeeded in a high degree"
(page 168).

"That is what Collins is mostly, just 'a wooden
show'"--a reference to a remark made by Anthony Trollope
in his Autobiography (entry 505)--"with marionettes pulled
about by wires that jingle and ring" (page 169).

(2.   Inclusions in Books ..., continued)

d.   DISCUSSIONS OF INDIVIDUAL WORKS

464   Brannan, Robert Louis.   "Introduction."   Under the
      Management of Charles Dickens: His Production of
"The Frozen Deep" [the play written by Wilkie Collins].   Ed.
Robert Louis Brannan.   Ithaca, N.Y.:   Cornell University
Press, 1966.
         Based on a dissertation by Brannan (entry 361 [and
616]).
         See entry 261 for annotation.

465   "The Moonstone," in "Four Mystery Reviews."   The
      Art of the Mystery Story: A Collection of Critical Es-
says.   Ed. Howard Haycraft.   New York: Simon and
Schuster, 1946.   pp. 379-380.
         Reprint of a review printed in the Athenaeum, July
25, 1868.
         The reviewer finds the characterization indistinct.
He praises The Moonstone.   The review seems silly.

466   Rycroft, Charles.   "The Analysis of a Detective Story."
      Imagination and Reality: Psycho-Analytical Essays
1951-1961.   London: Hogarth Press, 1968.   (International
Psychoanalytical Library, no. 75.)   New York: International
Universities Press, 1968, with the title, Imagination and
Reality.   xi + 143 pp.   "References": pp. 136-139.   Indexed.
         Introduction by M. Masud R. Khan and by John D.
Sutherland.
         Reprinted from the Psychoanalytic Quarterly (see
entry 561 for annotation).

467   Shaw, [George] Bernard.   "The New Magdalen and the
      Old."   Dramatic Opinions and Essays With an Apology.
Volume One.   New York: Brentano's, 1928.   Pp. 219-227
(total book length: xxv + 449 pp.).   No index.   Also printed

in: Our Theatre in the Nineties. Volume I. London: Constable and Company, 1932. Pp. 230-237 (total book length: viii + 288 pp.). Three volumes, with index in third volume.

Reprint of a review of a performance of the play, The New Magdalen, from The Saturday Review (entry 562).

The play was revived at the Theatre Metropole in October 1895.

Shaw finds the central character, Mercy Merrick, unrealistic. The play is old-fashioned by 1895's standards. Nonetheless, the play is superior to most contemporary 1895 drama.

The reprint of Shaw's article in Brentano's 1928 version cuts out the last half of his final paragraph.

468   Stebner, Gerhard. "Wilkie Collins: The Woman in
        White. " Der englische Roman im 19. Jahrhundert:
Interpretationon: zu Ehren von Horst Oppel. Ed. Paul
Goetsch, Heinz Kosok, and Kurt Otten. Berlin: E. Schmidt,
1973. Pp. 180-198 (total book length: 346 pp.). Bibliographies: pp. 318-346.

An appreciation of The Woman in White. Stebner's approach seems mundane.

469   Thomson, H. Douglas. Masters of Mystery: A Study
        of the Detective Story. London and Glasgow: Collins,
1931. Reprinted: Folcroft, Pa. : Folcroft Library Editions,
1973. 288 pp. Indexed.

A very brief discussion of The Moonstone. Silly.

470   Tillotson, Geoffrey. "Wilkie Collins's 'No Name. '"
        Criticism and the Nineteenth Century. New York:
Barnes and Noble, 1951. London: University of London,
Athlone Press, 1951. Chapter IX, pp. 231-243 (total book
length: ix + 283 pp.). Indexed.

A critical discussion of No Name. Tillotson's remarks are favorable. He finds that Collins may sacrifice too much in the way of believable characterizations and probability in order to construct an elaborate plot. Nonetheless, the novel's action and fascination can reward a reader.

This is a rare attempt to fathom the workings of a novel by Collins other than The Moonstone or The Woman in White.

471   West, Katharine. "Mid-Victorian. " Chapter of Gover-
        nesses: A Study of the Governess in English Fiction
1800-1949. London: Cohen and West Ltd. , 1949. Chapter
III, pp. 87-147 (total book length: 263 pp.).

Collins's No Name is discussed on pages 105-108.
West evaluates the character, Miss Garth, the governess in No Name. She finds Collins's "details of everyday life" (page 105) convincing. She then evaluates Norah, once under the care of Miss Garth, who becomes a governess.

"All Wilkie Collins's material on governesses ring true" (page 107).

West praises Collins's emphasis on the "human relationship" (pages 107-108) when portraying his governesses, and his realistic handling of the governesses.

472   "The Woman in White. " The Woman in White by Wilkie
        Collins.   Ed. Anthea Trodd.   Boston: Houghton Mifflin
Company, 1969.   Pp. 503-510.
        In "Appendix B. "
        Reprint of a highly favorable and interesting review
from The Times, October 30, 1860.   See entry 251.

(2.   Inclusions in Books ... , continued)

e.   INFLUENCES ON COLLINS

473   Chapman, Raymond.   "Realism and Sensation. "   The Vic-
        torian Debate: English Literature and Society: 1832-
1901.   London: Weidenfeld and Nicolson, 1968.   Pp. 171-
180 (total book length: 377 pp.).   "Bibliography": pp. 356-
367.   Indexed.
        On pages 175-177, Chapman briefly discusses Collins's development as a writer.   Chapman's remarks, while brief, are of interest.   He emphasizes Collins's character and personal life and their relationship to Collins's successes and failures in his writings.
        Collins is mentioned elsewhere in the book.

        Davis, Earle.   "The Collins Myth. "   The Flint and the
        Flame (1963).   See entry 479.

474   Murch, A. E.   "Detective Themes in the Works of
        Charles Dickens and Wilkie Collins. "   The Development
of the Detective Novel.   Philadelphia: University of Pennsylvania Press, 1958.   Reprinted: New York: Greenwood Press,
1968.   Chapter VI, pp. 92-114 (total book length: 272 pp.).
"General Bibliography": pp. 258-259.   Indexed.
        Murch writes that Collins's "novels of crime detection--

the only ones by which he is remembered today--owed a
great deal to Poe and even more to certain French sources"
(page 103).   He cites Maurice Méjan's Recueil des causes
célèbres (1807-1814) and Balzac as French sources.   He
attributes "A Terribly Strange Bed" to an experience of
Vidoeq, a French detective, in Vidocq's Mémoires.   Murch
also describes a case in Mejan's work which resembles the
plot of The Woman in White (page 107).
        This is a sympathetic and useful discussion of Col-
lins's fiction.   It is especially helpful for its discussion of
Collins's French sources.
        Collins is mentioned elsewhere in the book.

475   Rudman, Harry William.   Italian Nationalism and Eng-
        lish Letters: Figures of the Risorgimento and Vic-
torian Men of Letters.   London: George Allen and Unwin
Ltd. , 1940.   New York: Columbia University Press, 1940.
(Columbia University Studies in English and Comparative
Literature, no. 146.)   Chapters 4, 5, and 6 (total book
length: 444 pp.).   "Bibliography":   pp. 385-436.   Indexed.
        Columbia University Ph. D. thesis, 1940.
        Collins mentioned three times, briefly.
        Rudman suggests that Agostino Ruffini was the proto-
type of Professor Pesca of The Woman in White (page 221).

476   Russell, Lady.   Swallowfield and Its Owners.   New
        York, London, and Bombay: Longmans, Green, and
Company, 1901.   xii + 362 pp.   Indexed.
        Illustrated.
        Russell attributes to stories about the Pitt diamond
the idea for The Moonstone (page 211).
        Collins is also mentioned in passing on page 303.

        Storey, Gladys.   Dickens and Daughter (1971).   See
        entry 416.

477   Wallace, Irving.   "Hardly Coincidental. "   The Fabulous
        Originals: Lives of Extraordinary People Who Inspired
Memorable Characters in Fiction.   New York: Alfred A.
Knopf, 1955.   Chapter VIII, pp. 259-317 (total book length:
xii + 317 pp.).
        The discussion of Collins begins on page 296 and
ends on page 305.
        Wallace discusses the life and background of Inspector
Jonathan Whicher, the often-suggested model for Sergeant
Cuff of The Moonstone.   He discusses the Road Hill murder,
also known as the Constance Kent case, which Whicher
solved through clever deduction.

(2.   Inclusions in Books ..., continued)

f.   COLLINS'S REPUTATION AND INFLUENCE

Buchloh, Paul G.   "Der viktorianische Detektivroman:
Dickens und Collins. "   Der Detektivroman (1973).   See
entry 439.

478   Chew, Samuel C. , and Richard D. Altick.   "Charles
Dickens, Wilkie Collins, and Charles Reade. "   The
Nineteenth Century and After (1789-1939).   New York: Appleton-Century-Crofts, 1967.   Chapter XXIII, pp. 1344-1354
(total book length: x + 1111-1605 + unnumbered notes + xl
pp.).   Indexed.   Volume IV of A Literary History of England.
(Second edition.)   Ed. Albert C. Baugh.   1967.   (First edition in 1948.)
"Dickens's shift from novels of humorous character
to novels of sensational intrigue was partly due to Collins'
precepts and example" (page 1353).
The discussion of Collins is extremely brief.

479   Davis, Earle.   "The Collins Myth" and "Dead or Alive?"
The Flint and the Flame: The Artistry of Charles
Dickens.   Columbia: University of Missouri Press, 1963.
Chapter X, pp. 183-196; Chapter XIV, pp. 283-303 (total
book length: 333 pp.).   Indexed.
Illustrated.
Chapter XIV, "Dead or Alive?":   discusses Dickens's
The Mystery of Edwin Drood.   Deals at length and in detail
with Collins's influence on the writing of Edwin Drood.   "The
key to any explanation of the mystery [Edwin Drood] must
take Collins into account" (page 288).   "One cannot help won-
dering whether Collins at some time or other did not mention
some case or plot situation which inspired whatever Dickens
was intending to do in Edwin Drood" (page 289).
Davis sees a strong resemblance between Collins's
The Dead Alive, or John Jago's Ghost (1873-1874) and Edwin
Drood.   "The resemblances of this story [The Dead Alive]
to Edwin Drood are so remarkable that one must conclude
that they either represent what Collins thought Dickens' in-
tentions were, or else they may be studied as evidence that
this is the way Collins would have finished Edwin Drood if
he had been writing it" (page 289).
Chapter X, "The Collins Myth":   "... one must as-
sume that Collins replaced Forster as Dickens' most intimate
friend.   It seems also natural to observe that Forster would

take dim view of the younger man's influence and that in the
biography he would imply that Dickens' later novels could
not be as good as those he had written in happier and more
moral days when he was listening to his good friend's advice
and improving his technique by making the changes Forster
had recommended" (page 188).

Discusses Dickens's influence on Collins's work,
such as No Name (pages 188-189).   Also discusses Collins's
influence on Dickens's work: "... Dickens' last novel, Edwin Drood, was a direct attempt to surpass The Moonstone ..."
(page 189).

Davis feels that Collins's influence is exaggerated--
especially the supposed negative influence (which he refutes
well)--and reveals Collins's influence in an objective manner.

Davis makes several other references to Collins in
his book.   He deals briefly with the dislike of Collins's influence
on Dickens on the part of critics, biographers, and members
of "The Dickens Fellowship" which unjustly resulted in the
downgrading of Collins in published works about Dickens.

480   Devonshire, M. G.   "The Sensation Novel: Poe, Wilkie
        Collins, Miss Braddon.   'Le Roman Picaresque':
George Borrow. "   The English Novel in France: 1830-1870.
New York: Octagon Books, Inc. , 1967.   Chapter XXIV, pp.
396-406 (total book length: xvi + 484 pp.).   "Index of Names
Mentioned": pp. 480-484.

"Wilkie Collins and Miss Braddon, " pages 399-402;
contains a brief but useful discussion of Collins's reception
in France.   Devonshire quotes from French reviews of Collins's work.   He concludes that Collins's work was popular
with the general reading audience in France, but was "de-
plored, for the most part, by reviews of literary taste ... "
(page 402).

Eliot, T. S.   "Wilkie Collins and Dickens. "   Selected
Essays (1932).   See entry 443.

Ellis, S. M.   "Wilkie Collins. "   Wilkie Collins, Le
Fanu and Others (1931).   See entry 444.

Gerould, Gordon Hall.   "Variations in Romance. "   The
Patterns of English and American Fiction (1942).   See
entry 445.

481   Graham, Kenneth.   English Criticism of the Novel
        1865-1900.   London: Oxford University Press, 1965.
viii + 148 pp.   "List of Periodicals": p. 140.   Indexed.

Mentions Collins briefly three times.

Cites criticism as examples of Collins's low critical repute as a novelist (his characterizations were thought to be poor) in the nineteenth century, on pages 98-99.

Haycraft, Howard.   Murder for Pleasure (1941).   See entry 447.

482   Ley, J. W. T.   "Wilkie Collins. "   The Dickens Circle: A Narrative of the Novelist's Friendships.   London: Chapman and Hall, 1918.   Reprinted: 1919.   Chapter 64, pp. 286-291 (total book length: 363 pp.).   Indexed.
       Illustrated.
       Ley acknowledges Collins's influence on Dickens, and Dickens's affection for Collins.   However, he finds Dickens's affection "somewhat difficult of explanation" (page 286).   He finds Collins's influence on Dickens to be bad, and he displays a strong dislike for Collins.   Nonetheless, Ley gives a brief account of Collins's place in Dickens's life, and though he openly draws on John Forster's biography of Dickens (entry 391) and Percy Fitzgerald's works (entries 388 and 389), he goes further than either man to establish Dickens's feelings for Collins.
       "It was not a friendship in the ordinary sense: he [Dickens] came under Collins's spell to a remarkable degree, and one of the most astonishing of literary facts is the influence which the younger man exercised over the art of one who was famous and the acknowledged first of living novelists before he himself had left school" (page 286).
       Ley is unwilling to draw the logical conclusions from the evidence he presents; that is, Collins was a likable man who had the qualities of character which could attract the friendship and professional collaboration of a literary genius, Dickens, and that Collins's work has qualities which were useful to other writers, such as Dickens.   Ley's evident dislike seems based on the inaccurate accounts of Fitzgerald, and, in any case, clouds his perceptions so much that he falls into dogmatic conclusions which contradict the very evidence he presents.

483   Liljegren, Sten Bodvar.   The Parentage of Sherlock Holmes.   Stockholm: Almqvist and Wiksell, 1971. (Irish Essays and Studies.)   22 pp.

484   Manheim, Leonard.   "A Tale of Two Characters: A Study in Multiple Projection. "   Dickens Studies Annual. Volume I.   Ed. Robert B. Partlow, Jr.   Carbondale and

Edwardsville: Southern Illinois University Press, 1970. London and Amsterdam: Feffer and Simons, Inc. , 1970. Pp. 225-237 (total book length: xiii + 302 pp.). Indexed.

Collins's role in the writing of The Lighthouse, No Thoroughfare, and The Frozen Deep is discussed on pages 226-229.

See Harry Stone's "The Unknown Dickens, " entry 485.

485   Stone, Harry.   "The Unknown Dickens: With a Sampling of Uncollected Writings. " Dickens Studies Annual. Volume I.   Ed. Robert B. Partlow, Jr. Carbondale and Edwardsville: Southern Illinois Press, 1970.   London and Amsterdam: Feffer and Simons, Inc. , 1970.   Pp. 1-22 (total book length: xiii + 302 pp.).   Indexed.

Collins is mentioned several times in this essay, which may be of interest to a scholar investigating Collins's collaborations with Dickens, especially on The Haunted House (All the Year Round, 1859).

See Leonard Manheim's "A Tale of Two Characters, " entry 484.

486   Walpole, Hugh.   "Novelists of the Seventies. " The Eighteen-Seventies: Essays by Fellows of the Royal Society of Literature.   Ed. Harley Granville-Barker.   New York: Macmillan, 1929.   Cambridge, England: Cambridge University Press, 1929.   Pp. 22-24 (total book length: xiv + 284 pp.).   Indexed.

Collins's influence on Dickens is portrayed as negative (page 29).

Praises Collins elsewhere in the essay.

487   Ward, Adolphus William.   Dickens.   (English Men of Letters.) New York: Harper, 1902.   vi + 222 pp. London: Macmillan and Company, 1902 (reprint of 1882 edition).   Reprinted: 1905 and 1908.   vi + 232 pp.   Indexed.

Some libraries may mistakenly list the book under the name of the general editor of the English Men of Letters series, John Morley.

Collins is mentioned several times as Dickens's close, "cherished companion" (page 125 in both editions). Collins's influence on Dickens is portrayed as generally positive, with Collins "teaching" as well as "learning" from Dickens (page 111, both editions).

"It is no unique experience that the disciple should influence the master; and in this instance, perhaps with the co-operation of the examples of the modern French theatre, which the two friends had studied in common, Mr. Wilkie

Collins' manner had, I think, no small share in bringing about a transformation in that of Dickens" (page 199, Harper edition; 201, Macmillan).
        Collins is not discussed in detail. Primarily interesting for its viewpoint toward the Dickens relationship with Collins--one which did not become the accepted scholarly viewpoint.

(2.   Inclusions in Books ..., continued)

g.   CORRESPONDENCE (Written by and Written to Collins)

488   Clareson, Thomas D.   "Wilkie Collins to Charles Reade:
        Some Unpublished Letters. " Victorian Essays, A Symposium: Essays on the Occasion of the Centennial of the College of Wooster in Honor of Emeritus Professor Waldo H. Dunn.   Ed. Warren D. Anderson and Thomas D. Clareson. Kent, Ohio: Kent State University Press, 1967.   Pp. 107-124 (total book length: xiii + 127 pp.).   "Index to the Essays": pp. 125-127.
        Clareson discusses the problems relating to Collins's letters to Reade, and quotes portions of the twenty-seven letters in the possession of Michael Reade.
        Reviewed in The Dickensian (entry 643).

489   Dickens, Charles.   The Letters of Charles Dickens.
        3 volumes.   Ed. Walter Dexter.   London: Nonesuch Press, 1938.

490   Dickens, Charles.   The Letters of Charles Dickens.
        Multi-volume.   Ed. Madeline House and Graham Storey. London: Oxford University Press, 1965- .
        Volume Three mentions Collins's work in footnotes. Future volumes will probably deal with Collins more extensively.

491   Dickens, Charles.   Letters to Wilkie Collins 1851-70.
        Ed. Laurence Hutton and Georgina Hogarth.   London: J. R. Osgood, McIlvaine and Company, 1892.   191 pp. Also: Letters of Charles Dickens to Wilkie Collins.   Ed. Laurence Hutton and Georgian Hogarth.   New York: Harper and Brothers, Publishers, 1892.   171 pp.   Reprinted: New York: Kraus Reprint Corporation, 1969.   171 pp.   New York: Haskell House, 1974.   191 pp.

Introduction by Laurence Hutton.

The Letters were selected by Georgina Hogarth, Charles Dickens's sister-in-law. She apparently expurgated some passages. Many of Dickens's letters to Collins are reproduced.

(2. Inclusions in Books ... , continued)

h. OTHER SCHOLARSHIP

492 Baker, Ernest Albert. History of the English Novel.
Volumes VII, VIII, and IX (of ten vols.). London: H. F. and G. Witherby, 1924-1939. New York: Barnes and Noble, 1968-1972.
Collins is mentioned often. He is discussed at length in volume VIII, on pages 191-201. Baker provides some historical background to Collins's works. He also briefly analyzes Collins's novel craft.

493 Burns, Wayne. "Charles Reade. " Victorian Fiction:
A Guide to Research. Ed. Lionel Stevenson. Cambridge, Mass.: Harvard University Press, 1964. Pp. 277-293 (total book length: vi + 440 pp.). Indexed.
Very brief references to Collins on pages 284-285 and page 289.
See Robert P. Ashley's "Wilkie Collins, " from the same book, entry 423.

494 Catalogue of the Collection of Modern Pictures, Water-Colour Drawings, & Engravings, of Wilkie Collins, deceased; portraits by G. Romney and others, the property of John Carwardine, Esq. , deceased; also, pictures from the collections of Lord Acton, and the Rt. Hon. E. Pleydell Bouverie, deceased; which will be sold by auction, by Messrs. Christie, Manson & Woods: February 22, 1890. London: William Clowes and Sons, 1890. 19 pp.

495/6 Chandler, Frank Wadleigh. The Literature of Roguery.
2 volumes. Boston, 1907. (Types of English Literature.) Reprinted: New York: Burt Franklin, 1958. (Burt Franklin Bibliographical Series, no. 9.)
Collins is mentioned very briefly on pages 406 (A Rogue's Life, 1856), 533, and 549.

497 Exman, Eugene. The House of Harper: One Hundred

and Fifty Years of Publishing. New York, Evanston,
and London: Harper and Row, Publishers, 1967. x + 326
pp. Indexed.
        Illustrated.
        Collins is discussed on pages 61-62 and on 263.
        "In honor of Collins' trip to America to give read-
ings from his works, the firm issued an Illustrated Library Edition [see entry 31] of his sixteen novels" (page
61).

498   Haycraft, Howard, ed.   The Art of the Mystery Story:
        A Collection of Critical Essays. New York: Simon
and Schuster, 1946. ix + 565 pp. Indexed.
        A collection of essays. Collins is mentioned many
times. Contains a review of The Moonstone from 1868 (see
entry 465).

499   Kingsmill, Hugh (pseud. for Hugh Kingsmill Lunn).
        The Sentimental Journey: A Life of Charles Dickens.
New York: William Morrow and Company, 1935.   246 pp.
Indexed.
        Collins mentioned briefly several times.

500/1 Phillips, Walter Clarke.   Dickens, Reade, and Collins:
        Sensation Novelists: A Study in the Conditions and
Theories of Novel Writing in Victorian England.   New York:
Columbia University Press, 1919. Reprinted: New York:
Russell and Russell, 1962.   230 pp. "Bibliography": pp.
223-230.
        Based on a dissertation (entry 619).
        "The School of Dickens" includes Dickens, Collins,
and Reade (page 109).   "'Sensation novel' was Victorian parlance for romance for the populace" (page 218).
        Phillips provides a good background and some in-
sight into Victorian attitudes toward popular novels.

502   Robinson, Edwin Arlington.   Untriangulated Stars:
        Letters of Edwin Arlington Robinson to Harry De
Forest Smith.   Ed. Denham Sutcliffe.   Cambridge, Mass.:
Harvard University Press, 1947. xxvii + 348 pp. Indexed.
        Illustrated.
        Collins's work (principally Heart and Science, 1882-
1883) is discussed briefly in a letter on page 12.

503   Saintsbury, George.   Nineteenth Century Literature.
        New York: Macmillan and Company, 1896.

Saintsbury derogates Collins. See entry 446 for a
reply by Thomas J. Hardy.

504   Stang, Richard. The Theory of the Novel in England:
      1850-1870. New York: Columbia University Press,
1959. London: Routledge and Kegan Paul, 1959. Reprinted:
1966. xii + 251 pp. Bibliography: pp. 225-244. Indexed.
      Collins is discussed several times.

505   Trollope, Anthony. An Autobiography. 2 volumes.
      Berkeley and Los Angeles: University of California
Press, 1947. London: Cambridge University Press, 1947.
(Reprint of Edinburgh: Blackwood, 1883, edition) xxii +
312 pp. Indexed.
      Introduction by Bradford Allen Booth.
      Collins is discussed briefly in places. Scholars
have made much comment on what Trollope says about Collins, George Eliot, and others. Trollope's remarks about
Collins have been misquoted and misrepresented, so a re-
searcher is well advised to examine Trollope's remarks for
himself, and not to rely on a secondary source.

506   Wölcken, Fritz. Der literarische Mord: Eine Unter-
      suchung über die englische und amerikanische Detek-
tivliteratur. Nürnberg: Nest Verlag, 1953. 348 pp. Indexed.
      Some libraries list this book with the author's name
spelled "Woelcken."
      Collins is mentioned many times.

PERIODICAL ARTICLES

1. BIOGRAPHICAL

507   Adrian, Arthur A.   "A Note on the Dickens-Collins
      Friendship. " Huntington Library Quarterly, 16 (February 1953), 211-213.
          This article is often cited by scholars.   Adrian endeavors to establish that Dickens and Collins drifted apart
because of Collins's younger brother Charles's illness, cancer.   Dickens fretted over his daughter Kate's marriage to
such an ill man.   Wilkie resented Dickens's evidently hostile
attitude toward Charles.   Adrian cites passages from Annie
Fields's diary and a letter from Georgina Hogarth (Dickens's
sister-in-law) to Annie Fields to support his thesis.   Dickens was apparently distressed by the strain of Charles's illness upon Kate.

508   Beard, Nathaniel.   "Some Recollections of Yesterday. "
      Temple Bar, 102 (July 1894), 315-339.
          A firsthand recollection of Collins by the son of Collins's physician, close friend, and sometime neighbor, Frank
Beard.

509   Carrick, T. W.   "Wigton. "   The Dickensian, 46 (June
      1, 1950), 161-162.
          A lengthy excerpt from Carrick's History of Wigton
(Cumberland).   See entry 379.
          Dickens was "a sort of god" to Collins (page 161).

510   Cutler, B. D.   "The Great Victorians Come to America" (part two).   Publishers' Weekly, 122 (December 17,
1932), 2256.

511   Dickens, Charles.   "An Amusing Letter from Italy. "
      The Dickensian, 33 (Autumn 1937), 243-244.
          A letter from Dickens to his sister-in-law Georgina
Hogarth.   According to "The Editor" (probably Walter Dexter),

portions of the letter were "suppressed" (page 243) when it was published in Letters of Charles Dickens (1880).
The letter mentions Collins.

512   Dickens, Charles, Jr.   "Reminiscences of My Father."
Windsor Magazine, 81 (December 1934), supplement.
See Dickens's Reminiscences of My Father, entry 382.

513   Elwin, Malcolm.   "Wilkie Collins: The Pioneer of the
Thriller."   London Mercury, 23 (April 1931), 574-584.
Reprinted in Victorian Wallflowers (entry 387).
Collins was "a writer of brilliant originality ... "
(page 574).

514   Hyder, Clyde K.   "Wilkie Collins and The Woman in
White."   PMLA, 54 (March 1939), 297-303.
Reprinted in Victorian Literature, edited by Austin
Wright (see entry 400).
Hyder pulls together the various pieces of evidence which point to Collins's mistress, Caroline Graves, as the original for the Woman in White.   He discusses John G. Millais's description of his father's and Collins's encounter with a mysterious woman (see entry 409), but is skeptical about the reliability of the description.
Hyder also discusses Collins's studies of French crimes, and he discusses Collins's personal experiences, and the relationship they both have to The Woman in White.
This is a concise, straightforward article.   Hyder does not pretend to have all the answers for the many intriguing mysteries The Woman in White presents the interested scholar.   The article is frequently cited as a source by scholars, and is generally regarded as a landmark in Collins studies.   However, much of it has been superseded by more recent scholarship.
"When all is said, it is as a story that The Woman in White has most interest.   It was the story-tellers--Scott and Cooper and Dumas--that Collins cared for most among novelists; and he usually chose to write in an unadorned style, relishing most such prose as that of Byron's letters. Since Collins himself belongs among the great story-tellers rather than among the great novelists ... " (page 303).
It is in this article that the facts of Collins's relationship with his mistress are first pieced together.

515   Hyder, Clyde K.   "Wilkie Collins in America."   University of Kansas Humanistic Studies, 6 (1940), 50-58.
Collins evidently enjoyed his American visit; a visit,

Hyder asserts, inspired by Dickens's success and pecuniary profit. Collins read "The Dream Woman" (1855; expanded for the readings) to most of his audiences. Reviewers were very concerned with the story's effect upon the purity of women in the audiences. However, "The Frozen Deep," specially rewritten from dramatic into narrative form, met with favor.

Reaction to Collins seemed ambivalent.

516   Lohrli, Anne. "Andersen, Dickens, and Herr von Müffe." The Dickensian, 62 (January 1966), 5-13.

A brief discussion of Andersen's stay with Dickens and his encounters with Collins. "The Bachelor Bedroom" (1859) and the character Herr von Müffe are discussed. Herr von Müffe is identified as Collins's fictional portrait of H. C. Andersen.

517   "Wilkie Collins." The Dickensian, 47 (September 1951), 171.

A note on Collins's residences in London.

2.   BIBLIOGRAPHICAL

518   Andrew, R. V. "A Wilkie Collins Check-List." English Studies in Africa, 3 (March 1960), 79-98.

This list is the most complete as of this writing. It is not detailed, but is nonetheless a very important contribution to bibliographical studies of Collins.

519   Ashley, Robert P. "The Wilkie Collins Collection." The Princeton University Library Chronicle, 17 (1956), 81-84.

The Collins materials in the Parrish collection.

520   Clark, Alexander P. "The Manuscript Collections of the Princeton University Library." Princeton University Library Chronicle, 19 (1958), 159-190.

Items by Collins on pages 164-170 and 184.

521   Ewing, Douglas C. "The Harper Archive at the Pierpont Morgan Library." Manuscripts, 20 (Spring 1968), 40-42.

522   Gordan, John D. "New in the Berg Collection: 1959-

1961. " Bulletin of the New York Public Library, 67
(December 1963), 625-638.
>Part I of a series.
>"Wilkie Collins, " pages 633-634.
>Gordan describes an amanuensis's manuscript of the
version of "A Terribly Strange Bed" (1852) used for Collins's
readings in America.   He also describes the autograph manuscript of The Black Robe (1880-1881).   The novel's manuscript
is heavily corrected, and was apparently intended to be published as a serial (as indeed it was, in The Canadian Monthly,
according to R. V. Andrew, entry 518) in twenty-six weekly
installments.

523   Gordan, John D.   "News of the Month: Berg Collection. "
>Bulletin of the New York Public Library, 54 (June 1950),
301-302.
>Gordan announces the acquisition of Collins's manu-
script for "I Say No": or, The Love-Letter Answered (1884).
The manuscript is heavily corrected by Collins.   The novel
was probably intended to be serialized; contrarily, Sadleir's
(entry 433) and Parrish's (entry 430) bibliographies indicate
that the novel was published only in book form.   Gordan
points to the periodical London Society as the likely serial
publisher, beginning with volume 45, number 265, January
1884.

524   Gordan, John D.   "Novels in Manuscript: An Exhibition
>from the Berg Collection. "   Bulletin of the New York
Public Library, 69 (May 1965), 317-319.
>"The Black Robe: By Wilkie Collins, " pages 323-324.
>The novel was originally published as "The Yellow
Mask" in Household Words (1855).   The story was expanded
into the novel-length piece of anti-Catholic propaganda.   The
story was influenced by Edgar Allan Poe.   The manuscript
is heavily corrected.

525/6 Hart, F. R.   "Manuscripts of Wilkie Collins. "   Prince-
>ton University Library Chronicle, 18 (1957), 85.

>Jutzi, Alan.   "The Library Has Acquired 400 Letters
>Addressed to Edward Smyth Pigott. "   Huntington Library
Quarterly (1972).   See entry 593.

527   "The Manuscript of Wilkie Collins' 'Poor Miss Finch. '"
>Princeton University Library Chronicle, 15 (1954), 164-
165.
>An addition to the Parrish collection.

528   Schulz, H. C.   "English Literary Manuscripts in the
      Huntington Library. "   Huntington Library Quarterly, 31
(May 1968), 251-302.
      "COLLINS, William Wilkie, " page 263.
      Schulz lists the following manuscripts: Armadale: A
Drama in Three Acts (1866), The Frozen Deep (1866), How I
Write My Books ("contemporary copy"), Miss Gwilt, a Drama
in Five Acts (1875), and No Name, a Drama in Four Acts
(1870).   These are printed copies with Collins's "corrections
and additions. "
      Schulz also lists a corrected proof of "The Haunted
Hotel" (1878), a partial holograph of Lady Callista, a Drama
in Four Acts and Five Tableaux (is this by Collins?), and a
partial holograph of The Woman in White, in a Prologue and
Four Acts.
      Reprinted, entry 436.

529   Thomas, Deborah A.   "Contributors to the Christmas
      Numbers of Household Words and All the Year Round,
1850-1867. " The Dickensian, 69 (September 1973), 163-
172.
      Collins is briefly mentioned as a collaborator with
Dickens on pages 169, 170, 171, and 172.   Thomas identifies
Collins's contributions to The Seven Poor Travellers (1854),
The Holly-Tree Inn (1855), The Wreck of the Golden Mary
(1856), and The Perils of Certain English Prisoners
(1857).

530   Thomas, Deborah A.   "Contributors to the Christmas
      Numbers of Household Words and All the Year Round,
1850-1867: Part II. " The Dickensian, 70 (January 1974),
21-29.
      Collins is mentioned and discussed throughout the
article.   Portions of The Haunted House (1859), A
Message from the Sea (1860), Tom Tiddler's Ground
(1861), and No Thoroughfare (1867) are identified as
Collins's.

531   Wing, Donald G. , and Donald Gallup.   "The Blum
      Library: From A'Beckett to Zangwill. " Yale Univer-
sity Library Gazette, 33 (1958), 41-43.
      Letters by Collins.

532   "'With Admiration and Love. '" Colby Library Quarterly,
      2nd series.   (1948), 85-108.
      This article lists and describes one hundred books

exhibited at the Colby Library.   Books by Collins are included in the list.

3.   ASSESSMENTS OF COLLINS'S
LIFE AND WORKS

533   Ashley, Robert P.   "Wilkie Collins and the American
      Theater. "   Nineteenth-Century Fiction, 8 (March 1954),
241-255.
      Ashley lists Collins's plays (sixteen of them) on page
255.
      "Wilkie Collins considered himself a born dramatist
forced by the low state of the English Theater to write novels"
(page 241).
      Ashley covers the production and critical reception
of Collins's plays staged in the U. S. A.

534   Ashley, Robert P.   "Wilkie Collins and the Detective
      Story. "   Nineteenth-Century Fiction, 6 (June 1951),
47-60.
      Ashley discusses the development of Collins's detec-
tive fiction.   He claims for Collins the credit for inventing
many of the genre's motifs and most fascinating twists of
plot.   Yet, Ashley says, Collins did not know he was pioneer-
ing the genre of detective fiction (page 60).

535   Ashley, Robert P. , Jr.   "Wilkie Collins Reconsidered. "
      Nineteenth-Century Fiction, 4 (March 1950), 265-273.
      "Perhaps no other English novelist of comparable
stature has been the victim of such misrepresentation and
slipshod scholarship as Wilkie Collins, chiefly because until
recently no one had made him the object of a major investi-
gation" (page 265).
      Ashley goes on to defend Collins against bad criticism.
He attributes to "Ardent Dickensians" (page 265) such as J.
W. T. Ley (see entry 482) and Percy Fitzgerald (see entries
388 and 389), who took "their cue from the jealous Forster"
(see entry 391), the responsibility for Collins's "low critical
repute in the early twentieth century" (page 265).
      Ashley maintains that Collins's work did not decline
as much in quality as some critics say, but that of Collins's
novels, "Not even the worst of them.   The Fallen Leaves,
is wretched, and the best, such as Heart and Science, possess
considerable merit" (page 266).   Ashley effectively refutes

assertions that Collins's work declined in popularity.
    He identifies The Woman in White, No Name, Arma-
dale, The Moonstone, and Man and Wife as Collins's "five
major novels" (page 268). He cites Collins's poor health as
the reason Collins's "creative energy" (page 269) declined,
and denies that social protest was the reason. The validity
of complaints that Collins could not create characters is
denied by Ashley.
    Ashley goes on to refute other myths and to assert
that Collins's influence on Charles Dickens was beneficial.
    This essay is still useful.

536   Athenaeum (September 28, 1889), 418. [Anonymous;
      no title.]
          "Melodrama was Wilkie Collins's forte, but he worked
better as a novelist than as a dramatist. "
          A balanced appraisal.
          Reprinted in Norman Page's Wilkie Collins, entry 369.

537   Bićanić, Sonia. "Writing for the Magazines: A Study
      Based on the Novels of the Cornhill Magazine (1860-
1880). " Studia Romanica et Anglica: Zagrabiensia, No. 13-
14 (July-December 1962), 13-30.
          Collins is discussed on pages 20-21.
          Bićanić implies that Collins came to think his stories
in units of length suitable for All the Year Round and had
trouble thinking in units of other lengths (page 20). She
briefly discusses the publication of Armadale.

538   Booth, Bradford A. "Wilkie Collins and the Art of
      Fiction. " Nineteenth-Century Fiction, 6 (September
1951), 131-143.
          Booth finds Collins's international success and twen-
tieth-century revival grounded in Collins's vigorous story
telling. He does not find Collins's work profound, but finds
it fulfills a need for "escape fiction" and "calls for a com-
bination of talents which are not always part of the repertoire
of novelists of more exalted purpose" (page 132). Booth in-
vestigates the background and structure of Collins's fiction.
He finds Collins's work to be good in many ways, but inferior
to Poe and others. He finds Collins short on talent in some
ways, but long on determination.
          This is a thoughtful essay. Booth's assertion of a Col-
lins revival is vague and open to dispute. The burst of critical interest in Collins in the early 1950's was essentially
a new interest, not the renewal of an old interest. An in-
vestigation of the publications of Collins's works in the

twentieth century will show that the works follow the same
dips and rises in popularity that mark the works of other
Victorian writers, and that most shifts in a steady decline
in popular interest in Collins's works are due to the vagaries
of the publishing industry.

539   Chartres, H. "Wilkie Collins." London Society, 56
      (November 1889).

540   Compton-Rickett, Arthur. "Wilkie Collins." The Book-
      man (London), 42 (June 1912), 107-114.

541   Eliot, T. S. "Wilkie Collins and Dickens." Times
      Literary Supplement, No. 1,331 (August 4, 1927), 525-
526.
         "Dickens's characters are real because there is no
      one like them; Collins's because they are so painstakingly
      coherent and lifelike" (page 525).
         For more notes and a list of reprints, see entry 443.

542   Johnston, W. J. "Wilkie Collins and the Novelists of
      the Day." Irish Monthly, 19 (April 1891), 206-208.
         Contrasts Collins with other Victorian writers.
         An extract from this article is published in Norman
      Page's Wilkie Collins, entry 369.

543   Koige, Shigeru. "Wilkie Collins--Seitan 150 Nen ni
      Yesete." Eigo Seinen, 120 (1974), 412-413.
         "Wilkie Collins--For His 150th Anniversary" (trans-
      lation from page 101 of the MLA International Bibliography
      for 1974).

544/5 Lang, Andrew. "Mr. Wilkie Collins's Novels." Con-
      temporary Review, 57 (January 1890), 20-28.
         "He [Collins] still remains a most conscientious, and
      careful, and ingenious constructor of plots, a writer with a
      respect for his art, and deeply concerned with its processes.
      We still find in him a man with an almost bitter sense of
      human unhappiness, a man whose favorite characters are at
      odds with the world" (page 20).
         Lang discusses general themes and traits in Collins's
      work. Some of Lang's evaluations are still of value, although
      some of his remarks might be vitiated by Victorian moral
      prejudices. He ranks The Moonstone and The Woman in
      White as Collins's best work. He praises No Name, but dis-
      likes Armadale and both Collins's "immature" and his "later"
      (page 25) works.

"'I have always held,' says Mr. Collins, 'the old-fashioned opinion that the primary object of a work of fiction is to tell a story.' This opinion will probably outlive most of our perishable institutions" (page 24).

Lang also discusses Collins's views about characterization.

MacEachen, Dougald B. "Wilkie Collins and British Law." Nineteenth-Century Fiction (1950). See entry 570.

546   Swinburne, Algernon Charles. "Wilkie Collins." Fortnightly Review, 46 (new series), 52 (old series) (November 1, 1889), 589-599.

"... [T]he most plausible objection that could be brought against his [Collins's] best books was that the study of Character and the modesty of nature must too surely have been subordinated, if not sacrificed, to the exquisitely mechanical ingenuity of so continuously intricate a plot" (page 592).

Swinburne ranks The Moonstone as Collins's greatest work (page 594). The book's merit is "indisputable" (page 594). He sees Dickens's "didactic fiction and reformatory romance" as a possible influence on Collins's later, and to Swinburne, generally inferior work (page 595).

However, according to Swinburne, Man and Wife, "The first and best of Wilkie Collins's didactic or admonitory novels, is so brilliant in exposition of character, so dexterous in construction of incident, so happy in evolution of event, that its place is nearer the better work which preceded than the poorer work which followed it" (page 595).

This is a vigorous examination of Collins's art in novels. Swinburne feels Collins's work will win favor in future generations (page 589 and page 599). He portrays Collins as a unique man the unfulfillment of whose genius came from imitating the unique work of Dickens. "... Dickens was not a Shakespeare, and though Collins was not a Dickens, it is permissible to anticipate that their names and their works will be familiar to generations unaquainted with the existence and unaware of the eclipse of their most shining, most scornful, and most superior critics" (pages 589-590).

This may well be the best of the early essays about Wilkie Collins.

The essay is reprinted in Studies in Prose and Poetry (entry 458) and Norman Page's Wilkie Collins (entry 369).

547 [Townsend, Meredith White]. Spectator, 63 (September
     28, 1889), 395-396.
          Townsend's authorship is assigned by Norman Page
in Wilkie Collins: The Critical Heritage, on page 249. This
article is reprinted in Page's book (entry 369).
          Attempts to form a critical judgment based on Col-
lins's best work: The Woman in White, No Name, The Moonstone, and Man and Wife.

548 Waugh, Arthur. "Wilkie Collins and His Mantle. "
     Academy Magazine, 62 (April 5, 1902), 364-365.
          No writer has replaced Collins in his role as story
teller.

549 Yates, Edmund. "The Novels of Wilkie Collins. " Tem-
     ple Bar, 89 (August 1890), 528-532.
          Yates was a longtime acquaintance of Collins's and
admirer of his work (see the "Bibliographic Essay").
          "... [T]he world is poorer for want of one of the
most fearless and honest fictionists who ever fed the public's
sensation hunger while seeking to influence the public's serious
sentiments" (page 528).
          A well-written article.
          Reprinted in Norman Page's Wilkie Collins (entry
369).

4. DISCUSSIONS OF INDIVIDUAL WORKS

550 Allbut, Robert. "Shall It Be 'The Frozen Deep'?" The
     Dickensian, 7 (August 1911), 220-221.
          A brief discussion of performances of The Frozen
Deep.

551 Anderson, Patrick. "Detective Story. " Spectator, No.
     7226 (December 23, 1966), 820.
          "The oddity of The Moonstone is that the diamond
itself scarcely matters, except as catalyst or symbol" (page
820c). "The novel contains little of Christianity and less,
for all its rich and titled people, of class" (page 820c).
          A favorable discussion of The Moonstone.

552 Ashley, Robert Paul. "Wilkie Collins's First Short
     Story. " More Books: The Bulletin of the Boston Pub-
lic Library, 23 (1948), 105-106.

Ashley discusses "The Twin Sisters," which was published in Bentley's Miscellany in March 1851.

553   C., A. E. B.   "Revival of 'The Frozen Deep.'"   The
      Dickensian, 30 (Spring 1934), 118.
      A short review of a November 30, 1933, production of the drama, The Frozen Deep.   The review includes a bit of discussion about the play itself.

554   "Charles Dickens's Acting in 'The Lighthouse.'"   The
      Dickensian, 5 (April 1909), 91-94.
      A reprint of an article from Illustrated Times, July 21, 1855, entitled "Private Theatricals at Campden House." The article describes a performance of Collins's The Lighthouse, with one illustration.

555   Kiser, David.   "No Lady."   Saturday Review of Litera-
      ture, 18 (July 30, 1938), 9.
      A letter to the editor.
      Kiser calls S. M. Ellis's Wilkie Collins, Le Fanu, and Others (entry 444) "hideous criticism."
      Kiser discusses the identity of the Woman in White. He says that Collins's mistress is the original Woman in White.

556   Lawson, Lewis A.   "Wilkie Collins and The Moonstone."
      American Imago, 20 (Spring 1963), 61-79.
      Lawson discusses dreams in The Moonstone and Collins's unusual--for a Victorian--honesty about sexual impulses. Lawson credits Collins with several insights into human psychology, which presage Freudian psychology.
      He provides a psychoanalytic discussion of The Moonstone.   He suggests "twentieth-century psychology may be the key to the door to his [Collins's] inner life that he [Collins] had deliberately locked" (page 77).
      Lawson's biographical details are unreliable.

557   "The Lighthouse."   The Dickensian, 46 (March 1, 1950),
      60, and frontispiece.
      A short mention of the problems reviving The Lighthouse.   Includes an illustration of the 1855 production.

558   McCleary, G. F.   "A Victorian Classic."   The Fort-
      nightly, 160 (new series), 166 (old series) (August
      1946), 137-141.
      Often cited as The Fortnightly Review.
      Discusses The Moonstone.   Remarks on Collins's stature as a novelist and his artistic achievement.

"Readers of The Moonstone will surely agree with
Dickens that its characterization is excellent" (page 138).
McCleary goes on to cite Franklin Blake and Sergeant Cuff
as "life like" (page 138) characters.

MacEachen, Dougald B. "Wilkie Collins' Heart and
Science and the Vivisection Controversy." The Victorian Newsletter (1966). See entry 571.

559 [Noble, J. A.] [Untitled.] Spectator, 62 (January 26,
1889), 120.
    Noble is assigned authorship of this article by Nor-
man Page in Wilkie Collins: The Critical Heritage, in which
an extract of the article is reprinted (entry 369).
    A review of The Legacy of Cain. Noble feels that
the novel is not up to Collins's standards.

560 Reed, John R. "English Imperialism and the Unacknow-
ledged Crime of The Moonstone." Clio (University of Wis-
consin), 2 (1973), 281-290.
    "Far from being merely a classic detective tale, The
Moonstone (1868) is a novel of serious social criticism, con-
veying its meaning through unconventional characters and historical allusion" (page 281).
    The "Unacknowledged Crime" is the English soldier's
theft of the Moonstone.
    Reed examines Collins's social comment in The Moon-
stone. He examines the Moonstone as a symbol of crime.
Reed does not fit the initial theft (the theft by the Englishman
is the second one) into his (Reed's) logic.

561 Rycroft, Charles. "A Detective Story: Psychoanalytic
Observations." Psychoanalytic Quarterly, 26 (1957),
229-245.
    A psychoanalytical explication of The Moonstone; and
then an examination of Basil and its relationship to The Moonstone. Rycroft finds hints of Collins's own psychology (i.e.,
his mind) in The Moonstone and Basil. Rycroft's approach
is sophisticated--he expressly avoids literary criticism and
the application of child psychology to adult figures, a frequent
mistake in psychoanalytic approaches to literature. However,
he asks his readers to make assumptions which are strongly
open to question, and makes an attempt to find Collins in the
works discussed, which is of dubious value. Some of his
notions about detective stories as a genre seem dated, even
by the standards of 1956.
    Reprinted, entry 466.

562   Shaw, [George] Bernard. "The New Magdalen and the
      Old. " The Saturday Review (November 2, 1895).
      Reprinted in Dramatic Opinions and Essays with an
Apology and in Our Theatre in the Nineties (entry 467 for
both).

563   "Types of Popular Fiction: The Fast, the Sensational
      and the Simple. " Times Literary Supplement, No. 1839
(May 1, 1937), 343-344.
      "... [T]he fact that 'The Woman in White' in three-
volume form went through seven reprints and a revised edition in the first year of publication should be proof sufficient
of its opportune appearance" (page 344).   The public was
ready for the sensation novel.
      Very brief mention of Collins.

564   "When Found--. " The Dickensian, 12 (June 1916), 143-
      144.
      A short note identifying Collins as the author of
"Sister Rose" (1855).   The note points out that American
publishers would lift works from Dickens's magazine, Household Words, and reprint those works under Dickens's name,
regardless of who the true author may be.

565   Wolfe, Peter.   "Point of View and Characterization in
      Wilkie Collins's The Moonstone. "   Forum (Houston), 4
(Summer 1965), 27-29.
      "Collins's interest for the modern reader is chiefly
historical ... " (page 27).
      "By not using her [Rachel Verinder] as one of his
narrator-observers, Collins does not develop all of his heroine's resources or give full scope to her powers of percep-
tion" (page 28).
      "Nearly all of them [the characters besides Rachel]
depend heavily on gesture, idiom, and idiosyncrasy" (page
29).
      "Instead of depth, Collins endows his characters
with characteristic mannerisms" (page 29).
      "Yet we would be unjust to deny him [Collins] a
fresh awareness of ethical conduct.   This awareness exhila-
rates the entire novel in the form of sincere respect for
human contingency and scorn for deceit, regardless of popular cause or social position" (page 29).

5.   INFLUENCES ON COLLINS

566   Ashley, Robert. "Wilkie Collins and a Vermont Murder
      Trial. " New England Quarterly, 21 (September 1948),
368-373.
          "The Dead Alive" (1873-1874) is based on "the trial
of the Boorn brothers for the murder of Russell Colvin at
Manchester, Vermont, in October and November, 1819" (page
368).   Ashley describes the murder trial as Collins would
have read about it.   He ranks "The Dead Alive" "high among
the Collins novelettes" (page 373), even though the American
setting in the story is unsuccessful.

567   Caracciolo, Peter. "Wilkie Collins's 'Divine Comedy':
      The Use of Dante in The Woman in White. " Nineteenth-
Century Fiction, 25 (March 1971), 383-404.
          Caracciolo identifies the Divina Commedia as the
main source of symbolism in The Woman in White.   The book
is suffused with allusions to the Divina Commedia.   Caracciolo maintains that the references to the Divina Commedia
contribute importantly to the development and impact of The
Woman in White.
          ". . . [A]lthough the woman in white has an important
symbolic role in Collins's novel, she is only one element in
a complex pattern of images.   I suggest that a more compre-
hensive source than Méjan [Méjan's Recueil des causes
célèbres], so far as imagery is concerned, lies in the Divina
Commedia" (pages 383-384).
          "What seems to have escaped critical notice is that
Collins employs a wide range of allusion in all his best
work . . . " (page 385).
          "The parallels with the Commedia are, admittedly,
too fragmentary in themselves to provide the novel with the
kind of epic structure which it would have had if the Dantesque
images were purposively combined with the other symbols of
The Woman in White.   But the form of the novel is plainly
less dependent upon plot than it is usually thought to be; its
development is as much by symbolic counterpoint as by linear
progression" (page 402).
          This last statement is a very important notion, which
if true opens up a wide range of Collins's art heretofore un-
suspected.
          "Instead of Dante's division of his meaning into the
literal, allegorical, moral, and anagogical, Collins uses his
imagery to hint at the connections between the familial, class,
and national themes, the suggestions of the divine in the
novel serving the cause of human freedom" (page 403).

568   Grierson, Francis. "Who Was the Woman in White?"
       John O'London's, 3 (August 11, 1960), 165.

569   Grubb, Gerald G. "Dickens' Editorial Methods. " Studies
       in Philology, 40 (January 1943), 79-100.
            Collins is discussed on pages 87-92.
       Through Dickens's letters to Collins, Grubb tries to
illuminate the method Dickens used to help Collins develop
as a writer.

       Lohrli, Anne. "Andersen, Dickens, and Herr von
       Müffe. " The Dickensian (1966). See entry 516.

570   MacEachen, Dougald B. "Wilkie Collins and British
       Law. " Nineteenth-Century Fiction, 5 (September 1950),
       121-139.
            MacEachen examines how Wilkie Collins uses law in
his works, and the legal cases behind the laws used; and he
examines how the law figures in Collins's attempts at law reform through his writing.
            "This popular Victorian novelist deserves at least an
honorable mention in the history of British legal reform"
(page 139).
            MacEachen discusses No Name, Man and Wife, and
Heart and Science, and identifies them as novels with purposes.

571   MacEachen, Dougald B. "Wilkie Collins' Heart and
       Science and the Vivisection Controversy. " Victorian
Newsletter, No. 29 (Spring 1966), 22-25.
            This article opens with a lengthy discussion of the
vivisection controversy in the Victorian age. Mid-way on
page 24, Collins enters the discussion. In the character Dr.
Benjulia, MacEachen finds Collins's attempt to show a once
reputable man demeaned by his own use of vivisection for
experimentation. "Wilkie Collins' Dr. Benjulia is, of course,
merely a melodramatic monster, a kind of scientific bogey-
man, the vivisector burned in effigy" (page 25).

572   Ousby, Ian V. K. "Wilkie Collins's 'The Moonstone'
       and the Constance Kent Case. " Notes and Queries, 21
(January 1974), 25.
            The Constance Kent case is sometimes known as the
Road Murder case.
            Inspector Adolphus Frederick Williamson, who as-
sisted in the Constance Kent case, was an avid gardner--just
as is Sergeant Cuff of The Moonstone. "Given Collins's

familiarity with the Constance Kent case, this resemblance between the fictional and the real-life policeman can hardly be accidental" (page 25).

573   Reeve, Wybert.   "Recollections of Wilkie Collins."
        Chambers' Journal, 9 (June 1906), 458-461.
            Reeve was an actor in Collins's plays, and a friend of Collins.   This article contains anecdotes about Collins's trip to the United States and about the trip to Paris during which he purchased Maurice Méjan's Recueil des causes célèbres.

574   Tillotson, Kathleen.   "Dickens, Wilkie Collins and the
        Suicidal Curates."   The Dickensian, 69 (September
1973), 173.
            Tillotson finds the original for Collins's image of surplices looking like "a cluster of neglected curates who had committed suicide, by companionably hanging themselves all together"--first published in the serial version of The Woman in White, but deleted from the later book editions (although it reappears in the Houghton Mifflin Riverside edition, 1969, entry 251)--in Dickens's Martin Chuzzlewit, when Mr. Pecksniff sees a surplice "which had very much the appearance of two curates who had committed suicide by hanging."   Tillotson seems to prefer Collins's version.

        6.   COLLINS'S REPUTATION AND INFLUENCE

a.   NINETEENTH CENTURY

        Ashley, Robert P., Jr.   "Wilkie Collins Reconsidered."
        Nineteenth-Century Fiction (1950).   See entry 535.

575   Colby, Robert A.   "'How It Strikes a Contemporary':
        The 'Spectator' as Critic."   Nineteenth-Century Fiction,
11 (December 1956), 182-206.
            Collins mentioned on pages 189 and 194.
            Wilkie was one of many writers who fell victim to the Spectator's bias against sensation novels.   His work fared badly in the magazine's book reviews.   However, Heart and Science received "exaggerated praise" (page 194).

576   Coolidge, Archibald C., Jr.   "Charles Dickens and Mrs.

Radcliffe: A Farewell to Wilkie Collins. " The Dickensian, 58 (May 1962), 112-116.
        Coolidge's reasoning is difficult to follow. He seems
to argue that Mrs. Radcliffe's works, not Wilkie Collins's,
influenced Dickens's murder mysteries in Dickens's novels.

577   Corrigan, Beatrice. "Antonio Fogazzaro and Wilkie
      Collins. " Comparative Literature, 13 (Winter 1961),
      39-51.
        Fogazzaro borrowed from Collins motifs, characters,
situations, and "a conception of destiny which was originally
peculiar to Collins, as far as I know, and was shared by no
other English or Italian writer of his era except Fogazzaro"
(page 40).
        Corrigan bases most of her article on Fogazzaro's
Malombra. She builds a strong case for Collins's influence
on Fogazzaro's works, and cites several works written by
each author. She concludes that Fogazzaro was the superior
artist.

578   Davis, Earle. "Charles Dickens and Wilkie Collins. "
      The Municipal University of Wichita Bulletin, 20 (June
      1945), 3-26.
        Examines Collins's influence on Dickens.

      Eliot, T. S. "Wilkie Collins and Dickens. " Times
      Literary Supplement (1927). See entry 541.

579   Ellis, S. M. "Wilkie Collins. " The Dickensian, 28
      (Winter 1931-1932), 42.
        Merely a quotation from Ellis's Wilkie Collins, Le
Fanu and Others (entry 444).

      Fielding, Kenneth J. "Dickens and Wilkie Collins. "
      The Dickensian (1953). See entry 589.

580   Hoerr, Willmer A. "The Case of the Sundry Sources. "
      Baker Street Journal, 22 (December 1972), 215-218.
        The Hound of the Baskervilles was influenced by,
among others, Collins.

581   Ley, J. W. T. "Wilkie Collins's Influence upon Dick-
      ens. " The Dickensian, 20 (April 1924), 65-69.
        "He [Collins] influenced Dickens enormously ... "
(page 66).
        "In some subtle way it seems as if Collins rather
patronized Dickens" (page 67).

Ley finds no influence of Dickens on Collins.

"What was Collins's influence? It drove Dickens along what I shall always hold must ever have proved a no thoroughfare for him. It drove him to mere laboriousness; it tended to suppress all his spontaneity" (page 68).

Ley finds Collins's influence on Dickens to be very negative.

Much of what Ley asserts is disputed (by Robert Ashley, among others). Recent scholarship refutes some of his beliefs. The article is interesting for Ley's viewpoint, but his reasoning leaves much to be desired.

582 Meisel, Martin. "Miss Havisham Brought to Book."
      PMLA, 81 (June 1966), 278-285.

Among other influences on Dickens's character, Miss Havisham, is the famous passage from The Woman in White, in which the Woman appears mysteriously on a road. "It is clear that this apparition, with its mysteriously significant gesture struck Dickens like a summons from his own imagination" (page 281a). Meisel also finds that Collins's character and Dickens's character both share a relationship to the Gothic (page 283, footnote 12).

An interesting and sophisticated discussion.

583 Mews, Siegfried. "Sensationalism and Sentimentality:
      Minor Victorian Prose Writers in Germany." Modern
Language Notes, 84 (October 1969), 776-788.

Mews discusses Collins's publications in Germany in the nineteenth century.

584 Milley, Henry James Wye. "The Eustace Diamonds
      and The Moonstone." Studies in Philology, 36 (October
1939), 651-663.

Milley suggests that Trollope borrowed the plot for The Eustace Diamonds from The Moonstone. Milley further suggests the The Eustace Diamonds satirizes The Moonstone. This borrowing from a work by Collins is "surprising" (page 654), since "Trollope disapproved strongly of Collins's method of novel-writing" (page 654), and of Collins's novels. Milley may exaggerate Trollope's dislike of Collins's work. There are hints in the extant biographical materials that indicate a closer relationship between Collins and Trollope's family than is commonly supposed (see Kenneth Robinson's biography, page 196 and elsewhere, for such hints--entry 370), and which Milley might not have had available for aiding his argument.

585 Milley, Henry James Wye. "Wilkie Collins and 'A Tale

of Two Cities. '"   Modern Language Review, 34 (October
1939), 525-534.
      Milley demonstrates the "probability" (page 526) that
Collins's drama, The Frozen Deep, was not the limit of Collins's influence on Charles Dickens's A Tale of Two Cities.
Milley first attempts to show that Carlyle's French Revolution
was an influence on Dickens's book only after Collins's "Sister Rose" had provided Dickens with a locale for his story.
Milley's reasoning is attractive and strong.

586   Nelson, Harland S.   "Dickens' Plots: 'The Ways of
     Providence' or the Influence of Collins?" Victorian
Newsletter, No. 19 (Spring 1961), 11-14.
      Nelson seems to misunderstand what is meant when
scholars refer to Collins's influence on Dickens. He describes
a Christian order in Dickens's later works, which he feels
precludes any influence by Collins.   However, scholars rarely
assert any influence by Collins in the realms of world-view,
just in terms of mechanics, inspiration, and imagery.
      Nelson's article is revealing and informative, but it
never confronts the crux of the issue it raises: that Collins
influenced Dickens's concern for plotting, beyond characterization.

587   Scott, James F.   "Thomas Hardy's Use of the Gothic:
     An Examination of Five Representative Works. " Nine-
teenth-Century Fiction, 17 (March 1963), 363-380.
      Collins and Reade are mentioned as possible influ-
ences on Hardy's sensation novels (page 369).
      Surprisingly little has been written about Collins's
influence on Hardy's work, especially his early work.

(6.   Collins's Reputation ... , continued)

b.   TWENTIETH CENTURY

588   Ashley, Robert P.   "Wilkie Collins and the Dickensians."
     The Dickensian, 49 (March 1953), 59-65.
      "Not only was Wilkie Collins for many years Charles
Dickens's closest friend, but he was also the only Victorian
novelist to influence Dickens's art and the only Victorian
novelist whom Dickens accepted as a collaborator.   For
these three 'crimes' Collins won the undying animosity of a
certain group of Dickens idolators" (page 59).

Percy Fitzgerald (entries 388 and 389) and his book, Memories of Charles Dickens, bear the brunt of Ashley's assault. Then Ashley takes on J. W. T. Ley (a remarkably easy task--Ley's opinions about Collins consistently lack factual substantiation--see entry 482).

"Unlike his [Collins's] detractors," Ashley concludes, "he has not ridden to fame on the coat-tails of Charles Dickens, but has earned his reputation by virtue of talents which Dickens himself envied" (page 64).

This is a blunt rebuttal of notions of Collins and his relationship to Dickens fostered by several critics and scholars throughout the first half of this century. Ashley's assault on the often unsubstantiated opinions is justified.

Ashley does a great service by bringing a controversy which had been covert for decades into the open. This article is important reading for anyone who seeks to understand the development of scholarship and criticism about Collins in the twentieth century.

See K. J. Fielding's reply, entry 589.

589   Fielding, Kenneth J. "Dickens and Wilkie Collins: A Reply." The Dickensian, 49 (June 1953), 130-136.

This is a reply to Robert Ashley's "Wilkie Collins and the Dickensians," entry 588.

A well-reasoned examination of the evidence of Collins's influence on Dickens's works. Except for Edwin Drood, Fielding finds little evidence that Collins influenced Dickens's works. He examines A Tale of Two Cities in particular.

Fielding casts doubt on whether Collins actually "supplanted" Forster as Dickens's friend (page 134). The key word is "supplanted."

Fielding concludes: "... it must be said that Collins's four best novels are undoubtedly admirable, but that this makes not the slightest difference to the problem of effect of his work on Dickens; that while Percy Fitzgerald was unquestionably unreliable, this seems an inadequate reason for attacking Forster; and that although the problem of their literary relations deserves a much closer study, it has still to be examined far more carefully before anyone can not only pronounce that Dickens 'paid Collins the ... compliment ... of emulation,' but that Collins was 'the only Victorian' to have 'influenced Dickens's art'" (page 136).

Fielding's even tone contrasts with Ashley's fiery phrases, but this article is ultimately open to rebuttal. The question of Collins's influence on Dickens has yet to be adequately resolved. However, Ashley's portrait of the authoritative view of Collins prior to 1950 is not directly addressed

by Fielding, who discusses Forster (entry 391) and Fitzgerald
(entries 388 and 389) only. The weight of evidence, on this
point, seems to be on Ashley's side.

590   "The Return of Wilkie Collins. " The Bookman (New
          York), 35 (August 1912), 571.
          "There are signs of a considerable revival of interest
of late in the books of Wilkie Collins.... "
          This may be the first of four decades of claims that
a Wilkie Collins revival was taking place.

                       7. CORRESPONDENCE
                (Written by and Written to Collins)

591   Dickens, Charles. "Selected Letters: (I) Dickens Gives
          Wilkie Collins Details of His Life. " The Dickensian,
      22 (January 1926), 51-52.
          A letter written by Charles Dickens to Collins, June
6, 1856.

592   Flower, D. "Authors and Copyright in the Nineteenth
          Century, with Unpublished Letters from Wilkie Collins. "
      Book Collector's Quarterly, 7 (July-September 1932).

593   Jutzi, Alan. "The Library Has Acquired 400 Letters
          Addressed to Edward Smyth Pigott, English Newspaper
      Owner, and Later, Examiner of Plays for the Lord Chamber-
      lain. " Huntington Library Quarterly, 35 (May 1972), 293-294.
          Edward Pigott was a close friend of Collins for many
years.
          Jutzi quotes from and describes Collins's letters.
          This article is cited incorrectly in some bibliogra-
phies.

594   Monod, Sylvère. "Une Amitié française de Charles
          Dickens: Lettres inédites à Philoclès Régnier (II). "
      Etudes Anglaises, 11 (juillet-septembre 1958), 210-225.
          See also Part One: 11 (avril-juin 1958), 119-135.

595   "MS. Letter. Recent Accessions. " Bodleian Quarterly
          Record, 7 (1932), 31.

596   Shusterman, David. "An Edward Lear Letter to Wilkie
          Collins. " Modern Language Notes, 71 (April 1956),
      262-264.

"The friendship between Edward Lear, the Victorian poet of nonsense verses, and Wilkie Collins, the novelist, has long been well-known" (page 262).

Shusterman presents a letter by Lear to Collins which was not "in the two volumes of Lear's published letters ... " (page 263). In fact, no letters from Lear to Collins were in the collected letters of Lear.

In the letter, Lear mentions his possession of books written by Collins.

8. OTHER SCHOLARSHIP

597   "Correspondent, From a. " "The Author to His Pub-
      lisher. " Times Literary Supplement, No. 2, 346 (Janu-
ary 18, 1947), 38.
      Collins is twice mentioned in passing (concerning his relationship to Bentley and Sons, the publishers).

598   Dexter, Walter. "For One Night Only: Dickens's Ap-
      pearances as an Amateur Actor. " The Dickensian, 36
(September 1940), 193-201.
      Reproductions of playbills for The Lighthouse (1855) and The Frozen Deep (1857), with some commentary on their production.

599   Maurer, Oscar. "'My Squeamish Public': Some Prob-
      lems of Victorian Magazine Publishers and Editors. "
Studies in Bibliography, 12 (1959), 21-40.
      Collins and others were affected by their publishers' desires to avoid offending people.

600   Oddie, William. "Dickens and the Indian Mutiny. " The
      Dickensian, 68 (January 1972), 3-15.
      The focus is, of course, on Dickens.   Discusses The Perils of Certain English Prisoners, a special Christmas number of Household Words (1857) collaborated on by Dickens and Collins.

601   Robinson, Kenneth. "Wilkie Collins. " Times Literary
      Supplement, No. 2, 449 (January 8, 1949), 25.
      A brief request for biographical materials which deal with Collins.

602   Ruer, Jean. "Charles Dickens, Wilkie Collins et The

Frozen Deep. " <u>Etudes Anglaises</u>, 23 (avril-juin 1970), 183-189.

603   Solomon, Barbara H.   "Conrad's Narrative Material in
       'The Inn of Two Witches.'"   <u>Conradiana</u>, 7 (1975), 75-
82.

       Solomon finds plot and structural similarities in Con-
rad's "The Inn of the Two Witches" (1913) and Collins's "A
Terribly Strange Bed" (1852).   She uses Collins's story to
illuminate Conrad's narrative techniques.

       Although her focus is on Conrad's work, Solomon's
article reveals some of Collins's approach to his craft.

604   Walsh, J.   "Dickens's Friend, Wilkie Collins. "   <u>Hobbies</u>,
       57 (September 1952), 130-132.

(Part II, cont.)

DISSERTATIONS

1. DEVOTED SOLELY TO COLLINS

605   Ashley, Robert Paul, Jr.   The Career of Wilkie Collins.
       Harvard University, 1949.
       A survey of Collins's writings, with histories and
backgrounds.

606   Brashear, Barbara Ann.   Wilkie Collins: From Novel
       to Play.   Case Western Reserve University, 1972.   147
pp.   See Dissertation Abstracts International, 33 (October
1972), 1675A.
       A study of seven plays which Collins adapted from
his novels.   Brahear finds that Collins had a flair for drama.
However, his novels did not adapt well into plays.

607   Brightman, William Lloyd.   A Study of The Woman in
       White.   University of Washington, 1974.   176 pp.   See
Dissertation Abstracts International, 36 (December 1975),
3724A.
       Brightman finds that the characters in The Woman
in White are Victorian conventions.   He labels the conventions.   His discussion of broad literary themes manipulated
in detail by Collins is interesting.

608   Davis, Nuel Pharr.   The Early Life and Literary Career
       of Wilkie Collins.   University of Illinois, 1955.   323 pp.
See Dissertation Abstracts, 15 (1955), 822-823.
       Davis describes Collins's gradual disillusionment with
middle-class values.   He credits Collins's writing of sensation
novels to Collins's love of the Parisian theater and the low
state of the English theater.   The close working relationship
between Collins and Dickens is emphasized.   Credits The
Woman in White with setting high standards, in the creation
of backgrounds, which writers have sought to match.
       See The Life of Wilkie Collins by Davis (entry 367).

609   Dennis, Roger W.   Wilkie Collins and the Conventions

134

of the Thesis Novel.   University of Alabama, 1973.
491 pp.   See Dissertation Abstracts International, 34 (November 1973), 2616A-2617A.
Dennis examines No Name (1863), Man and Wife (1870), The Fallen Leaves (1879), The Black Robe (1881), and Heart and Science (1883).   He discusses what Collins's didactic purposes do to his plots, characters, and other elements of the novels.   Dennis finds more literary merit in Collins's thesis novels than is usually found in such novels.

610   Dunham, D. Dean, Jr.   The Growth of Wilkie Collins' Craftsmanship: "Antonina" to "The Moonstone" (1850-1868).   University of Nebraska at Lincoln, 1969.   334 pp. See Dissertation Abstracts, 31 (July 1970), 384A.
This is a study of Collins's first eight novels, Antonina (1850), Basil (1852), Hide and Seek (1854), The Dead Secret (1857), The Woman in White (1859-1860), No Name (1862), Armadale (1864-1866), and The Moonstone (1868). Dunham uses Collins's own critical criteria from the prefaces to Collins's novels, as well as other critical criteria, to evaluate the novels.

611   Heldman, James McDaniel, Jr.   Wilkie Collins and the Sensation Novel.   University of North Carolina at Chapel Hill, 1967.   378 pp.   See Dissertation Abstracts, 28 (March 1968), 3637A-3638A.
Heldman discusses the variety of approaches Collins used in his work.   Heldman also discusses Collins's characters.   He identifies and classifies various aspects of Collins's work.

612   MacEachen, Dougald B.   Wilkie Collins: Victorian Crusader.   University of Cincinnati, 1948.
MacEachen discusses Collins's social criticism.

613   Milley, Henry James Wye.   The Achievement of Wilkie Collins and His Influence on Dickens and Trollope.   Yale University, 1941.   283 pp.   See Dissertation Abstracts, 28 (April 1968), 4182A.
This is one of the most highly regarded of the dissertations on Collins.
Milley traces Collins's rise and decline as a novelist. He traces Collins's influence and popularity.   Collins's influence on Dickens's last four novels and on Trollope is discussed.   Collins's craftsmanship is also examined.

614   Sehlbach, Hans.   Untersuchungen über die Romankunst von Wilkie Collins.   Jena, 1930.   Published; see entry 371.

2. NOT DEVOTED SOLELY TO COLLINS

615   Baker, Donald Whitelaw. Themes of Terror in Nine-
     teenth Century English Fiction: The Shift to the Inter-
nal. Brown University, 1955. 428 pp. See Dissertation
Abstracts, 16 (1956), 118-119.
          Collins is discussed frequently, but is one of many
writers discussed.

616   Brannan, Robert Louis. The Frozen Deep: Under the
     Management of Mr. Charles Dickens. Cornell Univer-
sity, 1965. 196 pp. See Dissertation Abstracts, 26 (March
1966), 5429.
          See Under the Management of Charles Dickens: His
Production of "The Frozen Deep" (entry 261).

617   Burton, Carl Taylor, Jr. The Hero as Detective.
     Columbia University, 1973. 349 pp. See Dissertation
Abstracts, 34 (November 1973), 2549A.
          Chapter VII discusses The Moonstone. Asserts that
the novel is concerned with the human mind.

618   Hoffeld, Laura Diamond. The Servant Heroine in 18th
     and 19th Century British Fiction: The Social Reality
and Its Image in the Novel. New York University, 1975.
259 pp. See Dissertation Abstracts International, 36 (December 1975), 3730A-3731A.
          Includes heroines in Collins's works.

619   Phillips, Walter C. Dickens, Reade and Collins, Sen-
     sation Novelists: A Study in the Conditions and Theories
of Novel Writing in Victorian England. Columbia University,
1919. Published; see entry 501.

Part III

SELECTED BOOK REVIEWS

1. REVIEWS OF EDITIONS OF COLLINS'S WORK
(Listed under titles of Collins's work, which are arranged
alphabetically)

THE DEAD ALIVE

620   B., A.   "Old-Time Thrillers." New York Times Book
      Review, (November 6, 1949), 20.
            Review of Murder by Gaslight, ed. E. C. Wagen-
knecht (entry 327).
            Refers to "an indifferent Wilkie Collins novelette ... "
(page 20). The reviewer appears to be uninformed.

621   Guilfoil, Kelsey. "Crime Tales in Victorian Setting,
      Place." Chicago Sunday Tribune: Magazine of Books,
(November 6, 1949), 3.
            Review of Murder by Gaslight, ed. E. C. Wagen-
knecht (entry 327).
            "'The Dead Alive' by Wilkie Collins, a novelette, is
so inferior to the author's other mystery stories that I must
question its inclusion."

THE FROZEN DEEP (drama)

The following are reviews of Under the Management of Charles Dickens, ed. R. L. Brannan
(entry 261):

622   Choice, 4 (September 1967), 696. [Anonymous; no
      title.]
            The Frozen Deep is "a ninth rate play."

623   Collins, Phillip. Dickens Studies, 3 (1967), 168-170.

624   Gardner, Harvey C. "Author on Stage." New York

137

Times Book Review, (October 8, 1967), 57.
    Mentions Collins briefly.

625 Robinson, John W.   "On Drama." Prairie Schooner,
     41 (1967), 349-350.
         Praises the book. Mentions Collins.

626 [Staples, Leslie C.] "The Editor." The Dickensian,
     63 (1967), 123-124.
         Highly favorable.

THE MOONSTONE (novel)

627 "Bookwright" [pseud.]. New York Herald-Tribune
     Books, (February 14, 1943), 22.
         Review of The Moonstone with a foreword by A.
Woollcott (entry 156).

628 College English, 6 (March 1945), 357.
         Review of the Everyman The Moonstone, introduction
by Dorothy Sayers (entry 167).
         Favorable.

NO NAME (novel)

The following are reviews of No Name, ed. H.
van Thal (entry 196):

629 Caracciolo, Peter. Catholic Education Today, 1 (No-
     vember-December 1967), 31.

630 "Exhumations." Times Literary Supplement, No. 3,416
     (August 17, 1967), 737.
         Praises the plot and characterization of No Name,
although "the end is outrageously coincidental."
         Suggests Armadale be added to the series of revived
novels, of which this edition of No Name is a part.
         Favorable.

631 Goode, John. "Minor Nineteenth-Century Fiction."
     Victorian Studies, 11 (June 1968), 534-538.
         "It is no good noting, for example, that Hardy imi-
tated Wilkie Collins in his earliest novels: we need to know
why Collins was, for a radical innovator such as Hardy, the
most important novelist at that moment, and this can only

come through a profound awareness of what Collins achieved
in fiction and why he was able to achieve it" (page 535).

Goode finds No Name is a text "which fully" repays
"close reading" (page 535). However, "... the Doughty Library is so full of misprints that no one can have any faith
in its textual authority" (page 536).

A negative review of H. van Thal's introduction and
editing; but a positive review on No Name, itself.

"No Name is a very remarkable novel ..." (page 538).

632   Thorpe, Michael. "Current Literature 1967: II. "
      English Studies, 49 (1968), 364.
          "No Name will pleasantly surprise those who have
enjoyed the barely superior Woman in White: it is an intricate piece of intrigue, brilliantly worked out" (page 364).
This sentence is the sum total of what Thorpe has to say
about No Name.

633   Willis, Katherine Tappert. Library Journal, 92 (April
      15, 1967), 1640.
          Very brief praise of No Name.

           TALES OF TERROR AND THE SUPERNATURAL
                (ed. H. van Thal) (entry 312)

634   Purcell, James Mark. Studies in Short Fiction, 10
      (Fall 1973), 435-436.
          Purcell argues that Bleak House influenced Collins's
stories.
          This is a good short evaluation of Collins's short
stories. Purcell views the stories in Tales of Terror and
the Supernatural as developmental; he pictures them as learning experiences for Collins's writing of The Moonstone and
No Name, as well as two other unnamed novels of the mid-
1860's (probably The Woman in White and Armadale).

               THE WOMAN IN WHITE (novel)

      The following are reviews of Novels of Mystery from
The Victorian Era, ed. M. Richardson (entry 236).

635   Farrelly, John. "Worth Reprinting. " New Republic,
      117 (August 4, 1947), 31-32.
          Farrelly calls Richardson's anthology "a good idea
gone wrong" (page 31).

"Wilkie Collins' novel is one of the most interesting of its time, and certainly of its genre, but it is already available in several inexpensive editions, not to mention that it gluts the second-hand book shops" (page 31)--the total of Farrelly's remarks about The Woman in White.

636   "Victorian Mysteries. " Times Literary Supplement, (October 20, 1945), 497.
          "The last chapters of 'The Woman in White' form a piece of writing of which almost any author might reasonably feel ashamed" (page 497).
          "In its own day 'The Woman in White' succeeded because of the interest taken in its characters, which still exhibit a breadth, directness and simplicity that prove arresting" (page 497).
          Negative view of The Woman in White.

2.   REVIEWS OF WORKS ABOUT COLLINS
(listed alphabetically by author)

ASHLEY, R. P.
Wilkie Collins (entry 364)

637   "English Novelist. " Times Literary Supplement, No. 2, 621 (April 25, 1952), 282.
          The reviewer feels that Ashley's book lacks "depth. " Weakly favorable.

638   Hill, T. W.   "The Late Wilkie Collins. " The Dickensian, 48 (June 1952), 114-116.
          Unfavorable review.
          Hill feels that Ashley's biography of Collins lacks life.
          When this review is compared to his review of Kenneth Robinson's biography (review, entry 678; biography, entry 370), Hill appears to contradict himself when discussing Collins's relationship with Dickens.   In this review, he intimates that Collins's work's decline began with Dickens's death in 1870; yet, in the other, while defending Forster, he asserts that Collins and Dickens saw little of each other for years before Dickens's death.   This does not allow for Dickens's death--and hence the loss of his influence--to affect Collins.
          Hill feels Ashley's book takes the joy out of reading Collins.   He also denies Ashley's assertion that Collins worked as an editor on Household Words (page 116).

639   McCleary, G. F.   Fortnightly Review, 171 (April 1952),
      285. (Old Series volume number: 177).
          Favorable.
      Writes of Antonia instead of Antonina.

640   R. , J.   Spectator, 188, No. 6456 (March 21, 1952),
      379.
          Favorable.

641   Webster, Harvey Curtis.   "Each in His Way Knew How
          to Tell a Story. " The New York Times Book Review,
      57 (November 9, 1952), 30.
              Webster finds Ashley's writing dull.   Very brief.
      Seems to like the book.

                        BRUSSEL, I. R.
      Anglo-American First Editions, 1826-1900 (entry 424)

642   "Bibliographical Notes: Priority and Piracy. " Times
          Literary Supplement, (December 14, 1935), 864.
              Favorable.   Some mention of Collins.

      CLARESON, T. D.   "Wilkie Collins to Charles Reade. "
      Victorian Essays, ed. Anderson and Clareson (entry 488)

643   S. , M.   The Dickensian, 65 (September 1969), 190-191.
          Favorable.

                        DAVIS, N. P.
          The Life of Wilkie Collins (entry 367)

644   Altick, Richard D.   "Artisan of 'The Moonstone. '"
          Saturday Review, (February 23, 1957), 21.
              "Long intimacy with Dickens was, in another sense,
      Collins's greatest misfortune; for every reader of a biography
      of Collins tends automatically to measure the lesser man's
      character and personality against that of Dickens" (page 21).
              Altick views Collins's relationship with his mistress
      as "disreputable, or at least disheveled ... " (page 21).
              "Nuell Pharr Davis has written a conscientious but
      pedestrian narrative" (page 21).
              Altick questions whether Davis contributes much
      beyond what Robinson had already written.
              Mildly negative.

645   Ashley, Robert P.   "Davis's 'Life of Wilkie Collins.'"
       Nineteenth-Century Fiction, 12 (December 1957), 248-
250.
       "Dr. Davis has not added significantly to our know-
ledge of the facts of Collins' life" (page 249).
       "One is tempted to conclude that his [Davis's] method
is not scholarship but clairvoyance" (page 250).
       "... [A] lively and readable biography which creates
a vivid picture of the man, his life, his works, his friends,
and the times in which he lived and worked" (page 250).
       A favorable review, with some reservations about
the extent of Davis's research (page 249) and the presentation of conjecture as fact (page 250).

646   Booth, Bradford A.   Victorian Studies, 1 (September
       1957), 93-94.
       Booth chides Davis for not mentioning the biographies
by Robinson (entry 370) and Ashley (entry 364).   He praises
Davis's handling of the relationship between Dickens and Collins.
       "Mr. Davis does make us feel how much of Wilkie
Collins' wild, dream-shadowed imagination went into his
novels" (page 93).
       "But Mr. Davis, it should be admitted at once, has
no startling biographical revelations" (page 93).   Hyder (entries 514 and 515) and Robinson (entry 370) have already
"set forth" all "the essential facts" (page 93).
       Booth praises Davis's "mastery of possible autobio-
graphical elements in the novels ..." (page 93).   However,
Davis is not entirely convincing.   Booth also has trouble dis-
tinguishing new letters from old ones in Davis's notes.
       Davis's "inferences" are "clever" but "unguarded"
(page 94); "... there is little that is new [in Davis's book]
and much that is subject to corrective interpretation" (page
94).
       Booth disagrees with some of Davis's assertions.

647   Ferguson, DeLancey.   New York Herald Tribune Book
       Review, (December 23, 1956), 3.

648   Hart, Francis Russell.   "Wilkie Collins and the Problem
       of Biographical Evidence."   The Victorian Newsletter,
No. 12 (Autumn 1957), 18-21.
       A well-written discussion of the good and bad quali-
ties a biography may have, with its focus on Davis's biography.
A carefully reasoned negative review.

649   Lane, Lauriat, Jr.   Modern Language Notes, 72 (November 1957), 549-550.
      Praises Davis's documentation.
      Lane states that Davis's portrait of the relationship between Collins and Dickens is "as close to the truth as we are ever likely to come" (page 550).   He criticizes the book's bibliography and index for incompleteness.
      The book "should remain, at least until the eventual publication of a full edition of Dickens' letters, the best life of Collins we have" (page 550).

650   Notes and Queries, 4 (new series), 202 (continuous series) (April 1957), 183.   [Anonymous; no title.]
      "Dr. Davis's knowledge of Collins obviously exceeds his understanding of the man, and so the central figure of the book is curiously remote from the reader.   Nevertheless, this is a competent biography" (page 183).
      Praises Davis's "discussion of the relationship between Collins's life and his books" (page 183).
      "Wilkie Collins was not a great novelist" (page 183).
      Favorable.

651   [Pearson, Hesketh].   "Victorian Man of Mystery. "
Times Literary Supplement, No. 2,865 (January 25, 1957), 48.
      Reprinted in altered form, without the review material and with added remarks, in Pearson's Extraordinary People (entry 411).
      ". . . [h]e [Davis] does not add greatly to our knowledge of the man [Collins], whose personality is more vividly sketched by Mr. Robinson" (page 48).

652   Stevenson, Lionel.   Journal of English and Germanic Philology, 56 (1957), 505-507.
      Stevenson sharply criticizes Davis for his failure to credit Kenneth Robinson (entry 370), and for technical errors and erroneous references.   Stevenson calls Davis's style "naive abrupt" (page 507), and criticizes textual inconsistencies.
      "It [Davis's book] will be consulted, however, for its full details of Collins's business transactions, its emphasis upon the connections between his stories and his personal life, and its interesting analysis of his relations with Dickens" (page 507).
      Stevenson finds Davis's book inferior to Robinson's.

653   Stone, Harry.   "Dickens and Wilkie Collins. "   Dickensian, 53 (May 1957), 112-114.

Stone finds Davis's book lacks balance.

"Mr. Davis constantly ignores such passages which contradict his theories" (page 113).

Stone concludes, "But by subordinating fact to thesis and conjecture he [Davis] has vitiated his work" (page 114).

654   Wagenknecht, Edward.   "Irregular Private Life of Victorian Novelist. " Chicago Sunday Tribune: Magazine of Books, (January 20, 1957), 9.

Wagenknecht complains that Davis does not document "some of his most startling statements.... " But, he adds, Davis does enlarge the information previously available about Collins.

Wagenknecht expresses a high opinion of Collins.

655   "Weird Wilkie. " Time, 68 (December 31, 1956), 62-63.

"Compared to his friend Dickens, the English writing colossus of the century, Collins was a minor Victorian, but in the sense that Marlowe is a minor Elizabethan alongside Shakespeare.   He was the best of the second-best ... " (page 63).

The reviewer calls Davis's book "intellectually skimpy, but as a personal history of Collins it is thorough ... " (page 63).

"Sherlock Holmes, Hercule Poirot and virtually all the professional detectives of crime fiction stem either from The Woman in White or The Moonstone" (page 63).

656   Wood, Frederick T.   English Studies, 38 (1957), 180-182.

Wood praises Davis for making Collins interesting, and praises Davis's book for "psychological insight" (page 181) into Collins's mind, and for the presentation of new "facts of Collins's life and his literary career ... " (page 181).

"Mr Davis's work is carefully written and fully documented" (page 182).

Wood points out errors in spelling, and questions the "Americanized spellings in quotations from manuscript and printed sources ... " (page 182).   He calls these and other problems "minor faults" (page 182).

Davis's book "has made a definite contribution to our understanding of Wilkie Collins, and incidentally also to one aspect of the mid-Victorian literary world" (page 182).

Strongly favorable.

DE LA MARE, W.   "The Early Novels
of Wilkie Collins. "   The Eighteen-sixties,
ed. J. Drinkwater (entry 442)

657 "The Eighteen-Sixties. "   Times Literary Supplement,
No. 1, 584 (June 9, 1932),   423.
De la Mare "writes this time a little disappointingly.
He tells us really very little about his professed subject, the
'early novels. '"

658 ffrench, Yvonne.   "Belles-Lettres. "   London Mercury,
26 (Octover 1932), 568-570.
Briefly discusses de la Mare's essay on page 570.

659 Notes and Queries, 163 (July 2, 1932), 17-18.
Praises de la Mare's essay highly.

660 Reid, Forrest.   "Seventy Years Ago. "   New Statesman
and Nation, 3 (June 25, 1932), 832.
The bulk of the review is devoted to de la Mare's
essay.
Favorable.

661 Trilling, Lionel.   "The British Sixties. "   Nation, 135
(September 28, 1932), 288.
Strongly negative review.
"But even the Royal Society cannot excuse the weari-
someness of Walter de la Mare ... " (page 288).
"This is the wine-tasting school of criticism at its
best and most boring" (page 288).

LEWIS, N.
A Visit to Mrs. Wilcox (entry 407)

662 John, K.   "Men, Women and Poets. "   New Statesman,
54 (November 2, 1957), 576.
Praises, very briefly, Lewis's essay on Collins as
"one of her best things ... " (page 576).

PAGE, N.
Wilkie Collins: The Critical Heritage (entry 369)

663 Choice, 11 (January 1975), 1634.   [Anonymous; no
title.]
Finds the book useful, but feels that Page is un-
comfortable with the book's material.

664 [Hulse, Bryan.] The Dickensian, 71 (May 1975), 114-
     115.
          Favorable review.   By "B. H. "

665 Shelston, Alan.   Critical Quarterly, 16 (Winter 1974),
     382-383.
          Favorable review of the book.   Less than favorable
view of Collins.

666 Stewart, J. I. M.   "From Mystery to Mystery. " Times
     Literary Supplement, No. 3, 783 (September 6, 1974),
953-954.
          Stewart discusses the possible influence contemporary
criticism may have had on Collins, and he discusses the
quality and character of the criticism.   He feels that the
death of Dickens, more than anything else, contributed to the
decline in the quality of Collins's work.   Without Dickens
Collins's "confidence disintegrated ... " (page 954).
          "Collins had no true mission, no real endowment ex-
cept to entertain" (page 954).

                    PARRISH, M. L.
     Wilkie Collins and Charles Reade (entry 430)

667 "Bibliography and Sales: Wilkie Collins and Charles
     Reade. " Times Literary Supplement, No. 2000 (June
1, 1940), 272.
          Favorable.

668 Randall, David A.   The Papers of the Bibliographic
     Society of America, 35 (Second Quarter 1941), 168-171.
          Very favorable.

                    PEARSON, H.
          Extraordinary People (entry 411)

669 Griffin, Lloyd W.   Library Journal, 90 (April 1, 1965),
     1704-1705.
          Mentions Collins.

670 Wordsworth, Christopher.   "Eccentrics All. " Manches-
     ter Guardian Weekly, 92 (February 4, 1965), 10.
          Briefly mentions Collins, "whose private life was a
barnyard. "

RAWNSLEY, H. D.
Chapters at the English Lakes (entry 412)

671   "Dickens and the Lake District. " The Dickensian, 9
(October 1913), 266.
        Discusses Dickens's and Collins's trip in Cumberland.

ROBINSON, K.
Wilkie Collins: A Biography (entry 370)

672   Ashley, Robert P. "Kenneth Robinson's 'Wilkie Collins. '"
Nineteenth-Century Fiction, 7 (September 1952), 124-131.
        Credits Robinson's biography with bringing Collins out
of the oblivion in which certain Dickensians had placed him.

673   Baker, Carlos. "A Piercing Scream . . . and a
Beautiful Woman in White. " The New York Times Book
Review, (March 23, 1952), 3.
        Highly favorable review.
        Compares Collins's "eerie atmospheres" favorably
with Poe's.
        Well-written review.

674   Bevington, M. M. South Atlantic Quarterly, 51 (1952),
616-617.

675   Ferguson, DeLancey. New York Herald-Tribune Book
Review, (April 6, 1952), 5.

676   "A Great Story-Teller. " Times Literary Supplement,
No. 2, 600 (November 30, 1951), 757-758.
        Favorable.
        "Wilkie Collins was not a great writer, but he had
a good, straightforward, workaday style that got over the
ground" (page 758).
        "What he [Collins] was, was a great story-teller"
(page 758).

677   Green, Benny. "Victorian Rake and Rebel. " Spectator,
No. 7645 (January 4, 1975), 16.
        "For Collins must surely be one of the strangest odd-
balls to turn up in all the annals of English literature, a
man so clearly born out of his time that it is nothing short
of miraculous that he made himself so comfortable inside the
horsehaired hothouse of Victorian society" (page 16).
        "But it is a pity that Collins should have ended up

as one of Dickens's two shadows, for he was a formidable
artist in his right.   There is no question that his astonish-
ing mastery of plot construction, a gift well exercised by
his need to resort to it in his chaotic private life, influenced
Dickens profoundly in the last few novels, until with Edwin
Drood, we find the great man actually writing a kind of super-
Collins novel" (page 16).

　　　Highly favorable to both Robinson's book and to Collins.

　　　A lively and provocative article.

678　　Hill, T. W.   "The Enigma of Wilkie Collins."   The
　　　Dickensian, 48 (March 1952), 54-57.
　　　"Moreover we know from Dickens's letters to Collins
that the younger man did learn and benefit much from the
experienced writer" (pages 55-56).

　　　"I cannot think that Mr. Robinson is quite fair to
John Forster, on the 'Bear' side of whose character he lays
some stress" (page 56).

　　　"One feels, on reluctantly putting it down, that here
is the standard biography of Wilkie Collins" (page 57).

　　　A very favorable review.   Some of T. W. Hill's
discussion has been superseded by more recent work.

　　　See Hill's review of Ashley's biography, entry 638.

679　　Kirby, John Pendy.   "Victorian Domestic Scene." Vir-
　　　ginia Quarterly Review, 28 (Autumn 1952), 613-617.
　　　Robinson's biography is discussed primarily on page
617.
　　　"It is clear in Mr. Robinson's discussion that Collins anticipated the development of modern realism in England in his frank treatment of sexual relationships ... " (page
617).

　　　"At last, more than sixty years after his death, here
is the essential Wilkie Collins" (page 617).

　　　Favorable.

680　　Lewis, Naomi.   "Sixty Years After."   New Statesman
　　　and Nation, 43 (January 26, 1952), 105.
　　　"Yet Collins himself, while making full use of its
workings, seems hardly at all infected by the deep, unreal-
ised, monstrous hypocrisy of the time [Victorian era], which
caused no doubt so much of Dickens's hysteria" (page 105).

　　　"Collins's humanity went further than the usual vague
and guilty sentiment.   His sympathy with servants, to whom
he gave for the first time a dignified and serious literary
role, was revolutionary at the time, and was not at all well
received" (page 105).

Some phrases in this review reappear in Lewis's "A Terribly Strange Tale" in A Visit to Mrs. Wilcox (entry 407). Favorable review.

681 McCleary, G. F. The Fortnightly, 171 (New Series), 177 (Old Series) (February 1952), 137-138.
McCleary praises both Collins and Robinson's book.

682 "Mystery Creator." Newsweek, 39 (March 24, 1952), 126-127.
Short summary of the book's contents. Makes no evaluation.

683 "Other Selected Reprints." Times Literary Supplement, No. 3, 795 (November 29, 1974), 1347.
Review states that Collins's "two illegitimate--and by then octogenarian--daughters were still alive" when Robinson's biography of Collins was first published (page 1347).
"No full-length biography has appeared since Wilkie Collins was first published ..." (page 1347). (Evidently the anonymous TLS reviewer is unaware of N. P. Davis's and R. P. Ashley's biographies--entries 367 and 364).
Short and favorable review.

684 Phelps, Robert. "The Real, Right Victorian." Nation, 174 (May 3, 1952), 434-436.
Phelps feels Collins was a man more adapted to Samuel Johnson's view of supreme rational faculties than to Victorian thought, and thus out of place in Victorian England (page 434). He calls Collins "the true, the model Victorian" (page 435). Collins's interest in materialism and his chaotic personal life are deemed typical of Victorians.
He sees Collins's work as a "revealing index to the nineteenth-century consciousness ..." (page 436), and eminently readable, though "not even of secondary value ..." (page 436).
A favorable review.

685 Sadleir, Michael. Spectator, (December 7, 1951), 788.

686 Wagenknecht, Edward. "New Value on Works by Wilkie Collins." Chicago Sunday Tribune: Magazine of Books, (March 30, 1952), 6.
Wagenknecht feels that Collins's "domestic life" and the uncooperativeness of Collins's "morganatic family" account for the delay in the production of a biography of Collins. He feels Collins's work had not "been valued as it

deserves, " in spite of T. S. Eliot (see entry 443) and W. de
la Mare (entry 442).
Highly favorable review.

687   Walbridge, Earle L.   Library Journal, 77 (March 15,
1952), 526.
"Admirable biography ... " (page 526).
Praises the book highly.   Very brief.

688   Winterich, John T.   "Dickens's Confrere. " Saturday
Review, (May 3, 1952), 20-21.
Winterich discusses Collins's life and work.   He
praises Robinson's book.   He praises Collins.

AUTHOR, EDITOR, ILLUSTRATOR INDEX

SUBJECT INDEX

This index is supplementary to the categories
which already divide this bibliography.

After Dark (short stories) editions 2, 32, 68, 266-270, 313
The Air and the Audience   see   "The Use of Gas in Theatres"
The Alchemist, by Ben Jonson   177
All the Year Round   388, 537;   Collins's writings for 363,
   529, 530, 537
America   see   United States of America
Andersen, Hans Christian   516
"The Angler's Story of the Lady of Glenwith Grange"   see
   "The Lady of Glenwith Grange"
"Anne Rodway" (story) editions 296-297;   evaluated 459
Antonina (novel) editions 3, 33, 66, 80;   in general 341;
   evaluated 610
Armadale (novel) editions 4, 34, 57-58, 81-85;   in general
   368, 424, 445, 528, 535;   evaluated 387, 544, 610;   publication of 537
art of Collins's works: 368, 434, 440, 441, 442, 446, 448,
   450, 452, 453, 455, 461, 470, 471, 492, 505, 513, 514,
   536, 538, 544, 547, 548, 558, 567, 609, 610, 611, 613,
   676, 677, 679, 680
autobiographical fiction of Collins: 367, 400, 407, 514, 555,
   561, 568

"The Bachelor Bedroom" (essay) editions 293;   in general
   516
Balzac 360;   influence on Collins 474
Basil (novel) editions 5, 35, 59, 86-89;   in general 341;
   evaluated 561, 610
Bentley and Sons (publishers): 597
Besant, Walter: 7
"The Biter Bit" (story) editions 271-272, 296-297, 312, 325,
   456;   evaluated, 459
Black and White (play), editions 258, 259

"The Black Cottage" (story): 271, 296-297

The Black Robe (novel) editions 6, 72; in general 522, 524; evaluated 609

Bleak House, by Charles Dickens Collins's influence on 443; influence on Collins 634

Blind Love (novel) editions 7, 77, 90-95, 355

"Blow Up with the Brig!" (story), editions 51, 288, 308, 312

"Bold Words by a Bachelor" (essay), editions 293

books owned by Collins: 366

"Brother Griffith's Story of a Plot in Private Life" see "A Plot in Private Life"

"Brother Griffith's Story of Mad Monkton" see "Mad Monkton"

"Brother Griffith's Story of the Biter Bit" see "The Biter Bit"

"Brother Griffith's Story of the Family Secret" see "The Family Secret"

"Brother Morgan's Story of Fauntleroy" see "Fauntleroy"

"Brother Morgan's Story of the Dead Hand" see "The Dead Hand"

"Brother Morgan's Story of the Dream Woman" see "The Dream Woman"

"Brother Owen's Story of Anne Rodway" see "Anne Rodway"

"Brother Owen's Story of the Black Cottage" see "The Black Cottage"

"Brother Owen's Story of the Parson's Scruple" see "The Parson's Scruple"

Byron, Lord: 514

Camus, The Rebel 448

"The Captain's Last Love" see "Mr. Captain and the Nymph"

Carlyle, Thomas 383, 585

Carmilla, by J. Sheridan LeFanu, editions 236

"The Cauldron of Oil" (essay), editions 293, 308

characterization in Collins's works: 421, 431, 434, 440, 441, 442, 449, 452, 456, 463, 465, 470, 471, 481, 535, 541, 544, 546, 558, 560, 565, 571, 607, 618, 636

childhood of Collins: 402a, 419

Collins, Charles: 409, 420, 444, 507

Collins, Kate see Dickens, Kate

Conrad, Joseph: compared to Collins 603

the Constance Kent Case: 477, 572

Cooper, James Fenimore: 360, 514

the critics and Collins: 341, 364, 453, 479, 480, 481, 515, 575, 666

Hardy, Thomas, influenced by Collins 445, 587, 631
Harper and Brothers (publishers): 393, 497
"The Haunted Hotel" (story) editions 12, 71, 279-281, 330-
    331; in general 528
The Haunted House editions 347; in general 530; the writ-
    ing of 485
Hayne, Paul Hamilton, Collins's correspondence with 358,
    360
health of Collins 358, 421, 535; eye affliction 373, 394
Heart and Science (novel) editions 13, 74, 113; in general
    341, 502, 570, 575; evaluated 535, 571, 609
Hide and Seek (novel) editions 14, 37, 60, 114-116; evalu-
    ated 610
Hogarth, Georgina: 372, 507, 571
The Holly-Tree Inn, in general 529
Holmes, Sherlock: 655
The Hound of the Baskervilles, by Arthur Conan Doyle, in-
    fluenced by Collins 580
Household Words 388, 564; Collins's writings for 363, 389,
    529, 530
"How I Write My Books" (essay) editions 281; in general 528
humor of Collins: 363

influence of Collins in general 445, 449, 655 [see also
    names of authors or works]
influences on Collins in general 492, 570 [see also names
    of authors of works]
"The Inn of Two Witches," by Joseph Conrad, compared to
    Collins's "A Terribly Strange Bed" 603
Innes, Michael, influenced by Collins 447
"I Say No" (novel) editions 15, 38, 78, 117-118; in general
    451, 523

Jezebel's Daughter (novel) editions 16, 76; in general 424
"John Jago's Ghost" see "The Dead Hand"
John Jasper's Secret, by Henry Morford, editions 119
Jonson, Ben, The Alchemist 177
"A Journey in Search of Nothing" (essay), editions 293

Kent, Mr.: 357

"The Lady of Glenwith Grange" (story), editions 266-268,
    283, 312
"Laid Up in Lodgings" (essay), editions 293

"A Queen's Revenge" (essay), editions 293

Radcliffe, Mrs.: 576
Rambles Beyond Railways (nonfiction), editions 198
Rank and Riches (play), performances 396
Reade, Charles in general 488, 501; bibliographies 425,
     430, 493; his death 360; influence on Thomas Hardy
     587
Reade, Michael: 488
The Rebel, by Camus: 448
Recueil des causes célèbres, by Maurice Méjan, influence
     on Collins 474, 573
"A Remarkable Revolution" (essay), editions 293
residences of Collins: 418, 517
Road Hill Murder see Constance Kent Case
"A Rogue's Life" (story) editions 28, 79, 298-307, 335;
     in general 424, 495
Ruffini, Augustino: 475

Sadleir, Michael, "Wilkie Collins, 1824-1889" 120
Saintsbury, George: 446
"Save Me from My Friends" (essay), editions 293
Sayers, Dorothy, influenced by Collins 447
scholarship about Collins, discussion of 364, 423, 535, 588,
     686
Scott, Walter: 360, 514
The Seven Poor Travellers, in general 529
"A Shockingly Rude Article" (essay), editions 293
short stories, in general 363, 368, 634 [see also titles of
     collections and individual stories]
"The Siege of the Black Cottage" see "The Black Cottage"
"Sister Rose" (story) editions 266-269, 309; in general
     564; influence on Charles Dickens 585
Smith, Elder and Company (publishers): 399
Sophocles, Oedipus Tyrannus 177
Stevenson, Robert Louis, Dr. Jekyll and Mr. Hyde 236
"A Stolen Letter" (story) editions 266-269, 312; evaluated
     459

A Tale of Two Cities, by Charles Dickens editions 335;
     influenced by Collins 585, 589
"Talk-Stoppers" (essay), editions 293
"A Terribly Strange Bed" editions 266-269, 308, 312, 313-
     315, 336-339; in general 522, 603

"The Yellow Mask" (story) editions 266-269, 316-323; in
general 524
"The Yellow Tiger" (story), editions 324
"Your Money or Your Life" (story), editions 342 [see also
"Mr. Cosway and the Landlady"]